Cambridge Elements ≡

Elements in Shakespeare and Pedagogy
edited by
Liam E. Semler
University of Sydney
Gillian Woods
Birkbeck College, University of London

SHAKESPEARE AND PLACE-BASED LEARNING

Claire Hansen
Australian National University

CAMBRIDGE
UNIVERSITY PRESS

CAMBRIDGE
UNIVERSITY PRESS

Shaftesbury Road, Cambridge CB2 8EA, United Kingdom

One Liberty Plaza, 20th Floor, New York, NY 10006, USA

477 Williamstown Road, Port Melbourne, VIC 3207, Australia

314–321, 3rd Floor, Plot 3, Splendor Forum, Jasola District Centre,
New Delhi – 110025, India

103 Penang Road, #05–06/07, Visioncrest Commercial, Singapore 238467

Cambridge University Press is part of Cambridge University Press & Assessment,
a department of the University of Cambridge.

We share the University's mission to contribute to society through the pursuit of
education, learning and research at the highest international levels of excellence.

www.cambridge.org
Information on this title: www.cambridge.org/9781009011471

DOI: 10.1017/9781009019620

© Claire Hansen 2023

This publication is in copyright. Subject to statutory exception and to the provisions
of relevant collective licensing agreements, no reproduction of any part may take
place without the written permission of Cambridge University Press & Assessment.

First published 2023

A catalogue record for this publication is available from the British Library

ISBN 978-1-009-01147-1 Paperback
ISSN 2632-816X (online)
ISSN 2632-8151 (print)

Cambridge University Press & Assessment has no responsibility for the persistence
or accuracy of URLs for external or third-party internet websites referred to in this
publication and does not guarantee that any content on such websites is, or will
remain, accurate or appropriate.

Shakespeare and Place-Based Learning

Elements in Shakespeare and Pedagogy

DOI: 10.1017/9781009019620
First published online: October 2023

Claire Hansen
Australian National University

Author for correspondence: Claire Hansen, claire.hansen@anu.edu.au

ABSTRACT: *Shakespeare and Place-Based Learning* explores the potential of place for enriching Shakespeare pedagogy. Positioning place as a complex, multiperspectival phenomenon with stories and voices of its own, this Element considers place a partner in the learning process. The opening section traces the development of place-based education, culminating in a conceptual framework for use in Shakespeare pedagogy. *Shakespeare and Place-Based Learning* then examines how regional Australian students understand place in the Shakespeare classroom and presents a new definition of place designed for literary studies. This Element also investigates the challenges and potential of outdoor Shakespeare education through a case study of outdoor theatre workshops. *Shakespeare and Place-Based Learning* culminates with a pedagogical model and practical activities. This model aims to develop a learner's sense of place in two ways: through deepening their authentic engagement with and knowledge of Shakespeare's texts and by expanding critical awareness of their environmental responsibilities.

KEYWORDS: Shakespeare, place, place-based learning, ecocriticism, Shakespeare pedagogy

© Claire Hansen 2023

ISBNs: 9781009011471 (PB), 9781009019620 (OC)
ISSNs: 2632-816X (online), 2632-8151 (print)

Contents

Meeting Place

In the sixth line of *Macbeth*, the first Witch asks her sisters: 'Where the place?' (1.1.6). While the time and location 'to meet with Macbeth' (1.1.7) are prioritised by the Witches, questions of place are not ones we frequently ask of ourselves or our students. This is a question which place-based learning (PBL) asks educators and learners to be cognisant of: 'where are we?' (Shannon & Galle, 2017: 5). Where is our place of learning and what meaning does it generate for the teaching and learning of Shakespeare?

For the Witches, place is inseparable from their characterisation – they are living proof that 'places make us' (Gruenewald, 2003b: 621). They are partly given form by the stormy weather and elemental disturbance of their meeting in 'thunder, lightning and in rain' (1.1.2). Their connection to the 'the heath' (1.1.6) is axiomatic to readers and spectators. Banquo's astonished reaction to the sight of the Witches instinctively reads them in relation to their place: in fact, his talk is all of place when he and Macbeth stumble upon the Witches, as he wonders 'How far is't called to Forres?' (1.3.39). Upon encountering the Witches, they appear as 'wild' as the weather they describe and 'look not like th'inhabitants o'th' earth, / And yet are on't' (1.3.40–2). Upon vanishing, they are interpreted by Banquo as 'bubbles' of the earth and by Macbeth 'as breath into the wind' (1.3.79, 82). In this way, the Witches embody the basic premise of place studies, which 'begins to unpick the separation implicit in the preposition *in* – and finds rather that we are *of* the landscape, indeed that we *are* the landscape' (Somerville et al., 2011: 1, emphasis in original). If the Witches teach Macbeth and Banquo anything beyond the duplicitous prophecies they convey, it is the potency of place and its centrality to their characterisation.

To a twenty-first-century educator, though, Shakespeare's *Macbeth* may appear quite distinct from the place in which it is taught and learned. This is in part because, as the place philosopher Edward S. Casey observes, 'we rarely accord to place any such importance' (2009: xiii). 'Other than as a collection of buildings where learning is supposed to occur,' observes David Orr, 'place has no particular standing in contemporary education' (1992: 126). This disjunction between play and place became clearer to me when I taught *Macbeth* in Far North Queensland, where students envisage the

Scottish heath of *Macbeth* in the Australian tropics. The contrast between literary setting and lived place emphasised a dissociation between the study of literature (like Shakespeare's plays and poetry) and the immediate physical environment in which that teaching and learning takes place. In *Shakespeare and Place-Based Learning*, I respond to this tension and document my pedagogical journey towards PBL.

For Alexander C. Y. Huang, the concept of locality is 'under-theorised' in Shakespeare studies, and 'it is important to consider, in dramaturgical terms, the dynamics between Shakespearean localities, the localities of the critics, and the localities where Shakespeare's works are (re)presented' (2007: 193). To this we could add the localities of educators and students. My emplacement, or in Casey's words, 'implacement' (2009: xiii) in Far North Queensland has brought to the fore questions of the relationship between the localities of lived place and literary text. Lynne Bruckner and Dan Brayton ask: 'What does the study of literature have to do with the environment? Can reading, writing about, and teaching Shakespeare contribute to the health of the planet? What is the connection between the literary and the real when it comes to ecological conduct, both in Shakespeare's era and now?' (2011: 2).[1]

These questions are generated by an ecocritical imperative which seeks to investigate how literary studies and education can play a role in moving towards a sustainable future. Using place within humanities pedagogy may assist with this goal, according to Margaret Somerville and colleagues, who advocate for using place as 'an important framework for an integrated educational curriculum' (2009: 6) which addresses environmental issues from a range of perspectives and across traditional subject boundaries, from science to English. Such an approach recognises that 'all education is environmental education' (Orr, 1992: 12). In explicitly invoking place to teach Shakespeare, we acknowledge that '*place matters*, both in the world and in the text' (Wyse, 2021: 19, emphasis in original). This incorporation of place into Shakespeare pedagogy can not only invigorate a learner's engagement with the text but deepen their understanding of place.

---

[1] Randall Martin and Evelyn O'Malley point out that this 'leaves performance out of the enquiry' (2018: 377), something this Element attempts to address through its integration of pedagogy with performance.

Place has been 'a constant theme in the history of Western thought since at least the first century AD' (Cresswell, 2015: 23). However, conventional epistemology in humanities disciplines has 'largely disregarded landscape as a platform for learning' and understood space and place as 'a passive stage or a backdrop', disconnected from social life and action (Mayne, 2009: 175). In the context of higher education, PBL is 'often underemphasized' (Shannon & Galle, 2017: 5) and its omission across disciplines teaches students that 'ecology is unimportant for history, politics, economics, society, and so forth' (Orr, 1992: 85). Even outdoor education has overlooked 'place' (Wattchow & Brown, 2011: 120). While we may recognise implicitly the importance of place, it is not until relatively recently that 'spatial studies' has blossomed (Casey, 2009: xxi). Place has attracted considerable attention in recent decades (Mayne, 2009: 175; Wattchow & Brown, 2011: 82) and has 'become a powerful theoretical construct in many disciplines' including literature (Gruenewald, 2014: 142). A subset of cultural studies, place studies focusses on new understandings of place and the relationship between cultures and environments (Somerville et al., 2009: 6). Spatial studies, according to Casey, 'are now a whole industry' in the humanities. 'A spatial turn has been taken, with dramatic and far-reaching consequences. At the heart of this turn has been a recognition of the formative presence of place in people's lives and thoughts. Place is now a prominent theme in literary theory, cultural geography, psychoanalysis, and architectural theory' (2009: xxi–xxii). Despite these developments, the spatial turn is yet to find a firm hold in many fields. In most cultural and educational theory, David A. Gruenewald argues that the environment 'continues to be neglected' (2014: 144) and Urszula Pawlicka-Deger observes that the intertwining of 'place and humanities knowledge has been largely unexplored' (2021: 321). In *Shakespeare and Place-Based Learning*, I connect this spatial turn to the teaching and learning of Shakespeare, building on ecocritical developments in this field through my focus on place.

However, we cannot begin to engage with place without respect for Indigenous peoples, without acknowledgement of systemic, pervasive racism in our constructions of place and without awareness of 'the profound race-work that happens through race-attentive pedagogy' (Dadabhoy & Mehdizadeh, 2023: 1). Culture, ethnicity, gender and class are 'part of the event of place'

(Casey, 2009: xxv). Place and identity are inseparable. 'Who we are affects what we study, and how', and just as 'social locations inform our scholarship and teaching' (Dadabhoy & Mehdizadeh, 2023: 14–15), *where* we are informs our identity and affects our learning. We cannot separate the 'who' and 'where' of our identities as learners and educators. As such, place-based Shakespeare must listen to and learn from urgent work in critical race studies and 'premodern critical race studies' (Hendricks, 2019), including the vital work supported by the #ShakeRace and #RaceB4Race movements in Shakespeare scholarship and in anti-racist pedagogy (Akhimie, 2021; Dadabhoy, 2020; Dadabhoy & Mehdizadeh, 2020, 2023; De Barros, 2019; Eklund & Hyman, 2019; Erickson & Hall, 2016; Hall, 1996; hooks, 1994; Joubin & Starks, 2021; Karim-Cooper, 2020, 2021; Sterling Brown, 2020; Thompson, 2021; Thompson & Turchi, 2021).[2] This is crucial in any place-based work because Australian researchers 'cannot begin to articulate a position about place without confronting the complex political realities of Indigenous/non-Indigenous relationships in place' (Somerville, 2010: 330). There is much to learn from Indigenous knowledges of place: 'Place has long been noted as an organising principle in Aboriginal ontologies and epistemologies' (Somerville, 2010: 330). This recognises the multiplicity of place, as it is perceived differently 'by different cultural groups who hold different ways of being and knowing' (Greenwood, 2013: 98–9).[3] When working with place as a pedagogical framework, we must acknowledge that places are sites of trauma, dispossession, erasure, loss and exile, as well as loci for the violence of colonialism. An 'important collective act' of PBL is 'the process of recovering and retelling those stories of country, of restorying the land' (Cameron, 2014: 300), reconstructing 'previously invisible place

---

[2] See also the Anti-Racist Shakespeare webinar series (2021–2): www.shakespear esglobe.com/seasons/anti-racist-shakespeare.

[3] While Gruenewald (now Greenwood) is a pivotal scholar in the field of PBL, some scholars have critiqued his work for its 'inherently colonizing framework', as he himself discusses (Greenwood 2019: 366). He espouses that PBL should work towards decolonisation: 'writings on place that fail to engage significantly with the difficult issues of colonization, indigeneity, and race can be viewed as reproducing and reinforcing the erasures and silences that surround white, settler cultures' (2019: 366–7).

stories' and generating 'new stories about place' (Somerville et al., 2009: 8–9). To enrich Shakespeare education through place, we must begin by acknowledging that place is not inherently a pedagogical force for good, and neither is it a neutral blank canvas upon which we can write our Shakespeare lessons. It is a palimpsestic, complex and dynamic agent that encompasses the traumas of our histories of racial conflict, of ecological crisis and of individual encounter. It is neither a simple nor a risk-free addition to the classroom, but that does not make it any less valuable as a means of deepening our understanding of Shakespeare.

What constitutes a 'place' for Shakespeare education? A reader might think immediately of a classroom, a theatre or the outdoors, from 'the microgeographies of the classroom' to neighbourhoods and cities, schools and states (Angulo & Schneider, 2021: 389). The meaning of place will be wildly different from one learner to another. Place is also more than a passive tool to be added to our pedagogical toolbox, ready for deployment. Thinking of place as a 'vehicle' may be anthropocentric rather than ecocentric and overlooks the voice of place itself (Cameron, 2014: 297; Greenwood, 2013: 98). Although scholars like Pam Bartholomaeus describe place 'as a key resource and catalyst for learning activities' (2013: 18), I give to place an agential role. Place-based Shakespeare engages place as an active partner in learning with its own stories (Demarest, 2015: 6) that we must learn to listen to. This partnership should be mutually beneficial: learners should consider whether their learnings are 'in the service of place, or whether the place is only in the service of the story they are constructing' (Cameron, 2014: 299).

Drawing on theories of place, ecocriticism and complexity theory, as well as the voices of Shakespeare students in northern Australia, I will embrace multiple interpretations of place, from the material to the imagined. *Shakespeare and Place-Based Learning* is not an evaluation of the 'best' places for learning Shakespeare but rather investigates how place is constituted through complex social, environmental and cultural interactions, and how this interplay can be engaged to enrich the teaching of Shakespeare – wherever we are. Section 1 tracks the development of PBL from its interdisciplinary origins into contemporary literary studies, considers PBL's intersections with anti-racist Shakespeare pedagogy and offers a seven-part conceptual framework for teaching place-based Shakespeare. Section 2 examines theoretical and learner understandings of place as a

REFLECTION IN PLACE

Throughout *Shakespeare and Place-Based Learning*, 'Reflection in Place' prompts at the end of each section will support you to progress your own place-based journey. These reflections, inspired by Ambereen Dadabhoy and Nedda Mehdizadeh's vignettes and reflections in *Anti-racist Shakespeare*, are designed to meet you where you are in your engagement with place and to facilitate critical reflection to foster your sense of place and place-based pedagogy. This acknowledges that sense of place is subjective and that PBL requires ongoing learning.

For this first 'Reflection in Place', I invite you to consider:

- Where are you?
- What stories of your place do you know?
- How might the 'where' of your pedagogical context inform your practice?
- How might place influence your pedagogy in ways that may not be immediately visible to educators or students?
- How might you already be doing place-based learning?

These questions are designed to stimulate preliminary reflection on an educator's sense of place. This works against a tendency for place to operate as a 'mere backdrop' (Casey, 2009: xiii) in our teaching and learning contexts by simply making place visible in our work as Shakespeare educators.

critical precursor to implementing place-based Shakespeare. From this data emerges a multipart definition of place designed for use in Shakespeare PBL. Section 3 documents my early experience with outdoor place-based Shakespeare and examines the challenges, limitations and learnings of these explorations. This section features reflections from 'Shakespeare on Site', a series of outdoor theatre workshops for high school students.[4] Finally, in

---

[4] All research was conducted with approval from James Cook University's Human Research Ethics Committee, ethics application IDs H7660 (2019–22), H7771 (2019–20) and H8409 (2021–2).

Section 4, I offer a model and practical examples of learning activities and assessment for place-based Shakespeare classrooms. These activities include site reading, outdoor education, community engagement and creative and virtual place-based activities. Throughout, PBL is considered as a means not only of enriching Shakespeare pedagogy but of improving our understanding of ourselves, our relations with human and more-than-human others and our ability to engage responsibly with the environment to support our learning and our world.[5]

The explicit integration of place as an agent in the learning process can enrich our understanding of Shakespeare in many ways and across scales: fostering a deeper critical engagement with the settings of his playworlds (textual analysis); developing our knowledge of early modern environments (new historicism); incorporating a learner's environment to connect to Shakespeare's works (presentism); using Shakespeare's plays as a lens by which to examine our own engagement with place (ecocriticism). My use of the concept is capacious but also critical. Place-based learning is by no means a silver bullet nor an entirely novel approach to Shakespeare: it is in some ways already embedded in our pedagogical practice, in our scholarly research and in our students' engagement with the text (in productive and problematic ways). This approach has challenges and limitations and is not 'a panacea for the economic, environmental, political, and social dilemmas that confront modernity' (Gruenewald & Smith, 2014a: 357). It offers an additional pedagogical practice to promote civic engagement and care for others and the environment (McInerney et al., 2011: 13) and to develop critical thinking and authentic engagement in Shakespeare studies. In an era when the human relationship to place has reached a crisis level, PBL aligns with ecocritical aims to illuminate the study of Shakespeare through place and to enrich our sense of place through teaching and learning Shakespeare.

---

[5] I choose the term 'more-than-human' because it is 'used critically to remind human geographers that the non-human world not only exists but has causal powers and capacities of its own' (Rogers et al., 2013).

1 Developing Place-Based Shakespeare Pedagogy

Place is always a fundamental part of our experiences. It shapes our lives – pedagogically and otherwise – in urgent ways. In the face of the ecological disasters wrought by climate change, 'place emerges as ever more important' (Casey, 2009: xxviii).

> Daily we are presented with news about global warming, climate change, rapid loss of endangered species, and devastating catastrophes of weather. In Australia the local and the global have powerfully intersected in ways that make attention to global/local issues of greenhouse gas emissions, climate change, drought, increasing problems of water scarcity and local negotiations about water use, an imperative. (Somerville, 2010: 327)

But place is not always, or even often, a feature of our teaching. Literary studies and the teaching of English have a role to play in the 'newly emerging field of place studies' as we seek to 'know place differently' (Somerville et al., 2009: 3) and to communicate the urgency of revisiting our relationship to it. By incorporating place into education, we recognise that as ecological crisis changes the world, so must we transform education (Gruenewald, 2003a: 312; Wattchow & Brown, 2011: 14).

This transformative aim stems from PBL's resistance to educational scholarship's neglect of the person–place relationship (Greenwood, 2013: 97). Place-based learning does not seek to focus on place *instead* of 'content and skills' but rather posits that places can improve engagement and understanding (Gruenewald, 2003a: 315). It enhances the relevance of pedagogy to our lived experience by asking learners and educators to pay attention to their 'braided cultural, ecological and ideological landscapes' (Greenwood, 2019: 363). On a superficial level, we can therefore define PBL with relative simplicity: 'The key concept of cutting-edge, place-based pedagogy is that student learning is enhanced when course content is grounded in a particular place of meaning' (Hagood & Price, 2016: 603). Despite this seemingly simple formulation, there is no one way to implement PBL. This is in large part because PBL builds on shifting ground: every educator and classroom will have a different sense of place, so there is no 'one-size-fits-all' approach. Place-based learning 'can take a wide range of forms' while also being simultaneously 'specific to particular locales', making generic models and prescriptive advice inappropriate (Smith, 2002: 593, 587; Wattchow & Brown, 2011: 28).

In their survey of PBL literature, Janice L. Woodhouse and Clifford E. Knapp identify five useful characteristics: 'it emerges from the particular attributes of place'; it is inherently 'multidisciplinary'; it is 'experiential'; it reflects 'an educational philosophy that is broader than "learn to earn"'; and 'it connects place with self and community' (2000: 4). More recently, Simon Beames identified six key 'assumptions' of PBL: it is about education; it involves all kinds of place (local, distant, urban, rural); it considers past, present and future; it can be used across the curriculum; it encompasses interactions between place, humans and ecosystems; and it requires 'dwelling' and 'responding' (2015: 28). These core components expand the kinds of place included in PBL, enable historicist and presentist approaches, welcome consideration of complex interactions between the human and more-than-human and prioritise a focus on embodied experience and reflection.

The Development of Place-Based Learning

This understanding of PBL has developed over decades, because as Gregory A. Smith reminds us, '[p]lace-based education is not a new phenomenon' (2002: 587; 2017). It emerged in the latter third of the twentieth century as a concept and practice apart from environmental education (Ball & Lai, 2006; Smith, 2017: 17). Its philosophical roots are much older, dating back to the US philosopher and educationalist John Dewey, nature studies and experiential learning (Azano, 2011: 2; McInerney et al., 2011: 5; Wallis et al., 2021: 154). Place-based learning tends to straddle disciplinary divides, emerging not from education but from human geography, eco-psychology, deep ecology and philosophy (Beames, 2015: 27). These interdisciplinary origins are evident in its implementation. Educators will quickly identify that many of its methodologies are not unique to PBL. Peter McInerney and colleagues note its 'eclectic nature', with exponents adopting ideas and approaches from other education traditions including situated pedagogy and critical pedagogy (2011: 5). Place-based learning has similarities or links with an extensive range of pedagogies, including phenomenology (Gruenewald, 2014: 143), 'experiential learning, contextual learning, problem-based learning, constructivism, outdoor education, indigenous education, environmental and ecological education, bioregional education, democratic education, multicultural education, community-based education, [and] critical pedagogy itself' (Gruenewald, 2003a: 309). It is aligned with project- and problem-based learning, civic education and education for sustainability (Demarest, 2015: 1; Smith & Stevenson, 2017). For Smith, unlike most educational reform movements, it has 'functioned more like a vision of educational possibilities around which people already attracted to teaching in this way have rallied' (2017: 12). As such, PBL is a broad church – multidisciplinary, nebulous and emergent.

One point of difference is important for understanding the development of PBL: 'its explicit focus on both human and natural environments and its concern about equity and social justice issues as well as environmental' (Smith, 2017: 1). This focus on environmental justice is apparent in Orr's 'ecological literacy', a key concept in developing place-centric education that responds 'to a moral ecological imperative' (Wattchow & Brown, 2011: 121). Orr identifies six core foundations for sustainable education and ecological literacy, the first and most famous of which is his recognition that '*all education is environmental education*' (1992: 90, emphasis in original). A central facet of PBL is thus its investment in environmental sustainability; from a PBL perspective, education of all kinds should develop environmentally responsible learners.

However, this may conflict with our educational systems. We teach Shakespeare within a complex system of standardisation, testing and accountability. In the current climate, teaching with place might seem like an indulgent novelty, and educators might reasonably ask: how can place help our students write their Shakespeare essays or pass their exams? Liam E. Semler refers to the behaviour of educational systems as 'SysEd', 'the increasingly systematised nature of the education sector and professional labour within it' (2017a: 9, 2017b, 2017c). PBL may have developed in response to this hyper-regulation and over-systemisation. 'In an era when teachers' work is being prescribed and, to a large extent, controlled through external accountability processes, such as centralised curriculum and high-stakes testing, a growing interest in place-based education represents a refreshing turnabout in educational practice at the school and district level' (McInerney et al., 2011: 3).

This tension between the potential of PBL and SysEd is visible across the globe (James & Williams, 2017: 58–9; Loh, 2018; McInerney et al., 2011). In corporatising and commodifying educational experience, SysEd actively thwarts place-consciousness (Gruenewald, 2003b: 642; Gruenewald & Smith, 2014c: xiv–xv). There are many SysEd-generated barriers to implementing PBL in Shakespeare classrooms, from grassroots barriers like lack of time, training and overcrowded curricula to administrative barriers like funding and conceptual barriers such as school practices (Evans et al., 2012: 124).[6] But just as SysEd might inhibit PBL, PBL presents a challenge to SysEd. 'Place-based education challenges all educators to think about how the exploration of places can become part of how curriculum is organized and conceived. It further challenges educators to consider that if education everywhere does not explicitly promote the well-being of places, then what is education for?' (Gruenewald, 2003a: 317). Despite systemic constraints, PBL has developed around the world.[7] Scholarship on PBL has largely emerged from the United States, feeding off 'the literary tradition of North American nature writing' (Wattchow & Brown, 2011: 120). It is seen more often in primary and secondary education than in tertiary studies, although John I. Cameron notes that reconnecting a 'sense of identity and place' (2014: 301) is also important for adult learners.

---

[6] For further challenges to the implementation of PBL, see Smith (2017: 18), McInerney et al. (2011: 9), Demarest (2015: 103), Marchant et al. (2019), Gruenewald (2003a: 317) and Cameron (2014: 303). For an excellent example of how system pressures and politics can challenge the implementation of PBL in northern Australia, see Smith and Stevenson (2017).

[7] For more on global implementations of PBL, from the United Kingdom to Bhutan, see Smith (2017).

Despite global uptake, PBL lacks a concrete terminology, even in its identification as method or philosophy. Sharon Bishop claims that the beauty of place-based work is its lack of 'a fixed definition' because it is specific to the place 'that produces it' (2004: 66). Greenwood (who previously published under Gruenewald) differentiates between place-based education as a 'movement' and a teaching methodology and place-conscious education as a 'philosophical and political orientation to the field', a way of 'being and knowing' (Greenwood, 2013: 94; 2019: 360). Related terms abound, including 'place-consciousness' and 'ecological education' (Wattchow & Brown, 2011: 20–1; Woodhouse & Knapp, 2000). Cameron coins the term 'place responsive' pedagogy, which is focussed on the intersection of the 'materiality of place', 'cultural meanings that have been storied into the place across time' by both Indigenous and non-Indigenous people, and 'the agency of teachers and students' (Cameron, 2014: 288–9; Renshaw & Tooth, 2017: 2, 4). The related approach of ecopedagogy (Day Fassbinder et al., 2012; Hung, 2014, 2021; Kahn, 2010; Misiaszek, 2018, 2020) overlaps significantly with PBL; however, at present these two fields seem peculiarly disengaged. In *Shakespeare and Place-Based Learning*, I use the term 'PBL' to accommodate variants of the concept and recognise different theoretical, philosophical and practical pedagogical approaches to a learner's relationship with place. My choice of 'learning' emphasises activity, the open-ended, ongoing nature of PBL and highlights the learner's sense of place.

Place-based learning has been accused of lacking theoretical rigour. Although scholars like Gruenewald, Somerville, Ball and Lai have produced critical pedagogies of place or conceptual bases for place-based practices (Ball & Lai, 2006: 271), critics have pointed to the under-theorisation of PBL and ecocritical pedagogy and its lack of empirical evidence (Garrard, 2010: 240–2; Gruenewald, 2003a: 317; 2003b: 642; McInerney et al., 2011). Throughout *Shakespeare and Place-Based Learning*, I integrate place theory with PBL, in addition to two key theoretical frameworks useful for Shakespeare pedagogy: ecocriticism and complexity theory.

Ecocriticism is already well-established in Shakespeare studies and pedagogy (Bruckner & Brayton, 2011; Egan, 2006, 2015; Estok, 2011; Laroche & Munroe, 2019; Martin, 2015; Munroe, 2015; Watson, 2008). An 'omnibus' term, ecocriticism comprises 'an eclectic, pluriform, and cross-disciplinary initiative' that explores 'the environmental dimensions of literature and other creative media in a spirit of environmental concern' (Buell et al., 2011: 418). Surprisingly, despite the similar tenets and practices of PBL and ecocriticism – including their shared acknowledgement of the power of place and the urgency of rethinking our relationships to place – these fields rarely explicitly intertwine in scholarship or practice, especially in literary studies and Shakespeare education. Although Greg Garrard uses the term 'place-based ecocritical pedagogy' (2010: 234), there is little scholarly dialogue between ecocritics and place-based education scholars. Ecological pedagogies are frequently siloed: 'teachers of ecocriticism and environmental education researchers largely seem to work in mutual unawareness of the field developing in close proximity to their own' (2010: 233). Garrard calls for evaluation of the relationship between environmental literary criticism, ecocritical theory, pedagogical models and ecoliteracy (2010: 242). Bertrand Westphal also identifies the need for further bridging work across fields, noting that ecocriticism is yet to directly address 'the spatial turn' (2011: xii; Wyse, 2021: 14). Further critical conversation between Shakespeare, ecocriticism and PBL – and other related fields like ecopedagogy (Gaard, 2009: 326) – is needed, supporting a contact zone that encourages dialogue without collapsing the distinctions of these fields. These philosophies, theories and approaches (place-responsiveness, place-consciousness, ecopedagogy, ecocriticism), while not synonymous, all circulate around a belief in the potency of place for pedagogy.

These approaches to embracing place in pedagogy also share another theoretical core. Place-based learning scholars, place theorists and ecocritics often espouse an implicitly complexivist model of understanding place as a complex phenomenon produced by interactions. In moving away from Cartesian binary divisions to a perception of 'complex networks of causation' (Orr, 1992: 144–5) and understanding people, cultures and places as 'inescapably interconnected in relational systems' (Gruenewald, 2014: 146), place-based pedagogies are inherently complexivist.[8] Complexity theory provides a framework for understanding how complex systems work. It recognises the way that interactions create and sustain open, dynamic

---

[8] Brief reference is made to complexity theory within PBL (Smith, 2017: 11; Smith & Stevenson, 2017: 90).

systems, and thus is relational, not substantialist (Hansen, 2017). Relationships, not content, are key to complex systems. Complexity theory has been extensively developed in education and pedagogy to explain learning processes and the structure of our educational institutions (Biesta & Osberg, 2010; Davis & Sumara, 2006; Mason, 2008; Morrison, 2002) and has also been used in reference to Shakespeare education (Hansen, 2017; Semler, 2013). A complexity theory framework may offer structural support to the introduction of PBL in Shakespeare classrooms, as this theory emphasises the value of unpredictability and the unexpected, which is compounded when place is introduced into 'the relational dynamic between teacher, learner and knowledge' (Somerville et al., 2011: 3). This may enable educators to counter some of the challenges of PBL.

Pedagogies of Place for the Shakespeare Classroom

How, then, to model a place-based approach to teaching Shakespeare? While there are many frameworks identified by PBL scholars, I have selected three key approaches to help inform *Shakespeare and Place-Based Learning*: Greenwood's critical pedagogy of place; Somerville's tripartite framework; and Beames' continuum of place-responsiveness. In Section 4, I build on these approaches to offer a practical model for place-based Shakespeare pedagogy.

The theoretical development of PBL is largely attributed to Gruenewald/Greenwood's critical pedagogy of place. Greenwood looms large in the development of PBL, particularly through his synthesis of critical pedagogy and place-based pedagogy to produce a 'critical pedagogy of place', which has been powerful in the subsequent development of the field. His work 'significantly deepened the theoretical underpinnings of place-based educational approaches' (Smith, 2017: 11–12). It has not been without criticism, however (Stevenson, 2008: 356; see the introductory section 'Meeting Place' and Note 3). Broadly, this approach centres on the historical question of 'what happened here?'; the socioecological question of 'what is happening here now and in what direction is this place headed?'; and the ethical questions of 'what should happen here?' and 'how to be here?' (Greenwood, 2013: 97; 2019: 364; Smith, 2017).

A critical pedagogy of place links to two mutually dependent aspects of ecological politics: decolonisation and reinhabitation. Decolonisation refers to culturally responsive teaching, resisting exploitation and oppression (Greenwood, 2013: 96; Gruenewald, 2014: 149). Reinhabitation refers to identifying, recovering and creating places and prioritises learning to live well in place (Greenwood, 2013: 96; Gruenewald, 2014: 149). It is the 'confluence' of cultural and ecological thinking that is central to Gruenewald's approach to PBL: the nexus of environment, culture and education is at the heart of his place-conscious pedagogy (2003a: 320; 2014: 147–8).

Building on years of collaborative place research with Australian Indigenous people, Somerville responded to Gruenewald's critical peda-gogy of place with her own proposal for postcolonial and feminist post-structural pedagogy of place (Somerville et al., 2009: 8). She articulates a tripartite conceptual framework for place pedagogy: 'our relationship to place is constituted in stories (and other representations); the body is at the centre of our experience of place; and place is a contact zone of cultural contact' (2010: 335). These three elements – story, body, contact zone – offer possibilities for 'generating place pedagogies for change' (Somerville et al., 2011: 4). Her emphasis on a contact zone where 'different stories can be held in productive tension' (Somerville et al., 2009: 9; Carter, 1992) is central to a complex understanding of place that respects diversity and multiplicity.

Beames' three-step PBL framework establishes a continuum of place-responsiveness, recognising different engagements with place and provid-ing steps for generating authentic PBL. The first step comprises three kinds of place-based education along a continuum of place-responsiveness. At one extreme is 'place ambivalent' PBL, which ignores place or treats it as a 'staging ground' for activities. Beames' example of this is 'doing a Shakespeare lesson outside because the sun is shining' (2015: 28–9). The second type of PBL is 'place sensitive'; this approach 'pays some attention to local phenomena'. The other end of the continuum is 'place essential', which 'describes learning that is directly related to the exact location in which it takes place' (2015: 28–9). Loh gives the example of 'learning about Shakespearean drama at the Globe in London' (2018: n.p.). Analysing practice through this continuum is the first level of Beames' model (2015: 29). The next step is to add a 'critical dimension' – like Greenwood's critical pedagogy of place – to lay the groundwork 'for people to transform their places' (2015: 29). The third step, 'critical cosmopolitanism', shows students how issues in their places are related to other places 'in a complex web of history, geography, politics and economics'. Beames' framework moves from place awareness to transformation (2015: 29).

These approaches inform my definition of PBL as learning with place as an active agent in the complex interactions of the classroom, with the aims of deepening learning about place (in all its historical, local-global, idiosyncratic complexities), developing a sense of place, supporting learning about the topic or subject of the class and encouraging learners to develop environmental responsibility. Will all of these occur in every PBL lesson? Ideally yes, but realistically no. Rather than a revolutionary place-based overhaul that replaces conventional education, 'small changes' are an ideal way to invite place-based approaches into a classroom (Demarest, 2015: 159).

Following Beames, PBL can be thought of as a spectrum: at one end is a heightened focus on place ('place as topic'), where the primary object of study *is* place; at the other end ('place as teacher'), place is used to better understand subjects (science, English) or objects of study (including literary texts). Amy B. Demarest identifies a similar distinction in looking at ways of enacting PBL (2015: 53, 56). There are limitations and challenges to both ends of this spectrum. The use of place for specific purposes can be exploitative (Wattchow & Brown, 2011: 133–4), while incorporating place in a lesson focussing on another topic may not, according to some, qualify as 'a fully fledged place-based study' (Demarest, 2015: 56). Authentic PBL must aim to incorporate both ends of this spectrum, engaging place as a teacher and topic in a two-way conversation that illuminates and benefits both partners (place and topic of learning).

In an ideal manifestation of PBL, 'reading literary texts in actual place can thus serve to mediate our understanding of place while deepening our understanding of texts read' (Loh, 2018: n.p.). In this optimal scenario, the benefits of PBL are twofold: it enables students to learn more about place, while using place to learn more about what they are studying. However, the nature of teaching and the nature of place mean that these variables are not always controllable. Place-based learning may sometimes be partial, incomplete or favour place as topic or teacher. Place-based Shakespeare pedagogy will always be a matter of degrees. Beames suggests that educators ask: 'to what degree can (and should) your place-education genuinely respond to the place in which it happens?' (2015: 30). In each classroom, the 'degree' will change. Imperfect PBL is inevitable and limitations to its implementation should not prevent educators from engaging with place in the teaching of Shakespeare. In fact, reflecting on the incompleteness of place-based practice is essential for the development of PBL. As I will show, my early experiments with PBL have developed my understanding of how place informs the teaching of Shakespeare. The things that go wrong, the restrictions that our various pedagogical contexts create and the idiosyncrasies of any learning environment can illuminate the role of place in our pedagogies, in Shakespeare's texts and in how we think of ourselves as educators and as people inhabiting stunningly diverse places across the globe.

Teaching Literature and Shakespeare with Place

The role of place in literary studies is changing. In 1997, Casey reflected that there was 'little said of place' in literary theory; in 2009, he acknowledged that 'place is now a prominent theme' in the discipline (1997: 12; 2009: xxi–xxii). Place is undoubtedly central to literature and literary studies (Green, 2013: 29; Loh, 2018). Literary texts do far more than simply reproduce place (Potter & Seale, 2020: 367): place and text exist in a bidirectional or 'symbiotic relationship' (Mundell, 2018: 1; Loh, 2018). Learners may even develop their representation of place *through* literary texts (Cormack & Green, 2007: 85–6). The 'spatial turn' is present in several ways within literary studies: through the rise of literary geography, literary cartography, geocriticism and ecocriticism (Mundell, 2018: 1; Estok, 2011; Potter & Magner, 2018; Prieto, 2011; Tally, 2011; Thompson, 2013; Wyse, 2021). Emily Potter and Kirsten Seale put forward the concept of 'the *worldly text*' as an alternative conceptualisation of the literature–place relationship (2020: 368, emphasis in original), while Lowell Wyse has developed a theory of 'ecospatiality' which shows how 'geospatial and ecological realities coincide with and inform literary representations' (2021: 13). In Shakespeare studies, there is significant scholarship on site-specific and outdoor Shakespeare theatre (Escolme, 2012; Gaby, 2014; Martin, 2015; Martin & O'Malley, 2018; Minton, 2018, 2020, 2021),[9] and in early modern literary studies a growing interest in place and space (Berry, 2016; Bozio, 2020; A. Hansen, 2021).

Although there is little systematic adoption of place in secondary English (Green & Clark, 2013: 2–3, 8), many scholars acknowledge the potential of PBL specifically for English education (Anae, 2013; Azano, 2011; Bishop, 2004; Fischer, 2015; Gannon, 2009a, 2009b; Koessler & Perduca, 2019; Loh, 2018), writing education (Bass et al., 2020; Donovan, 2016; Lindholdt, 1999), theatre and drama pedagogy (Monk et al., 2011) as well as literacy studies (Charlton et al., 2011; Cormack & Green, 2007; Green & Clark, 2013; Green et al., 2007; Wyse et al., 2012). The uses of PBL in literary studies take various forms for different purposes. In Australia, Susanne Gannon challenges pejorative associations of place (2009a: 29). In Singapore, Loh explores local literature through local place (2018). In Argentina, Cecilia Koessler and Florencia Perduca argue that, through PBL, literary texts can develop students' 'spatial thinking skills', spotlight literary themes and offer students 'a new form of perspectivism' (2019: 115, 123). In the United States, Sarah Fischer's PBL practice reinforces 'the importance of imagination' (2015: 13).

While there is no established body of scholarship on PBL in Shakespeare education, Nicole Anae provides a unique example in her work on teaching Shakespeare in Oceania, where she explored the reciprocity between drama, the politics of place and identity (2013: 122). The lack of Shakespearean PBL is perhaps because some place-based advocates argue that local texts should be prioritised (Ball & Lai, 2006: 279). While local culture is central to PBL, to assume knowledge of what constitutes 'local' for our learners and to exclude all non-local texts would be an unnecessarily limiting way of implementing PBL in Shakespeare classrooms. All texts are 'literally and/or imaginatively situated in a place' (Kern, 2000: 10, 11) and thus are ripe for

---

[9] For an important recent example, see 'Cymbeline in the Anthropocene', www .cymbeline-anthropocene.com/.

PBL. While local texts enable learners to see their places anew, imaginative literature enables students 'to look within themselves and re-imagine what their roles in those places could be' (Fischer, 2015: 23). Place-based approaches are thus suitable for any kind of literary text, including Shakespeare.

Place and Anti-racist Shakespeare Pedagogy

While any Shakespeare classroom can implement place-based pedagogies, this must be done with awareness of and respect for the places where this teaching occurs and our learners' sense of place. Australia – where I live – is today dominated by attitudes that often appear the antithesis of place-responsiveness. White settlement has marginalised Indigenous Australian culture, which is profoundly integrated with Country. Indigenous Elder Aunty Joan Tranter explains the significance of 'Country':

> Australia's Indigenous peoples are direct descendants of hundreds of different Indigenous language groups and Aboriginal countries in Australia, each with their own particular place referred to as 'my Country', 'my mother's Country' or 'my father's Country'. In saying this, we are referring to land known as *Country* with which each family or language group has held traditional custodianship and responsibilities that have been passed down through hundreds of generations over many, many thousands of years. We have held these responsibilities to our lands to ensure their spiritual, cultural and economic survival since time began. The land is the source of our identity. Although nowadays many of us may no longer live on our traditional lands and Country, we are still very much connected to it. (Tranter, 2013)

Indigenous identity and culture are inseparable from place or Country. However, since white settlement, Indigenous peoples have suffered incomprehensible damage to their relationships with Country, due to loss of land and identity, interruptions to oral traditions, fragmentation of communities, forced displacement, stolen generations, intergenerational trauma, dislocation and loss of kinship knowledge (Lowan-Trudeau, 2018: 513–20). Australia has not only forcibly separated Indigenous peoples from Country but also produced 'one of the worst records of land and water degradation and loss of biodiversity, and an economic system that treats place in terms of development potential and private property rights' (Cameron, 2014: 288). And Shakespeare's canon is inextricably bound up in the ideologies that have shaped countries like Australia: 'Shakespeare and his works reproduce those white, European, imperialist agendas' (Dadabhoy & Mehdizadeh, 2023: 9). How, then, can we create place-based learning experiences that acknowledge and respect the traumatic, violent histories of oppression embedded in place while teaching the works of an icon of the imperialist agenda behind it? In teaching place-based Shakespeare, we must recognise not only the positioning of whiteness as 'that which is most human' (Dadabhoy & Mehdizadeh, 2023: 9) but also the racial positioning of place. Shakespeare's plays position place – from setting to the figurative use of place and space – from a perspective of whiteness. Shakespeare's own 'imperialist fantasy' (Dadabhoy & Mehdizadeh, 2023: 9) inflects his representation and interpretation of place.

Place-based approaches to teaching and learning Shakespeare must engage with anti-racist pedagogy and listen to and respect Indigenous perspectives on PBL (Lowan-Trudeau, 2018; Scully, 2012; van Gelderen, 2017). Anti-racist pedagogy seeks to 'effect social transformation' (Dadabhoy & Mehdizadeh, 2023: 12) and in this way aligns with the goals of PBL. Both require critically understanding and challenging the complex operations of power, and both approaches recognise the importance of intersectionality. But, at present, there remains 'a persistent absence of explicit Indigenous voice' and a lack of 'personal examples from Indigenous perspectives' in literature on critical pedagogy of place (Lowan-Trudeau, 2018: 512, 513).

There are several anti-racist models for PBL, including A. M. O. Trinidad's 'Critical Indigenous Pedagogy of Place' that advocates for 'Indigenization' instead of Greenwood's 'decolonization' (Trinidad, 2014: 111–12; Lowan-Trudeau, 2018: 513–14; Trinidad, 2011, 2012, 2014). In Australia, Tyson Yunkaporta proffers a valuable 'eight-way Aboriginal Pedagogy Framework' to assist educators to incorporate Aboriginal knowledge in the classroom (2009: 45–6). While challenging for non-Indigenous educators, embracing Indigenous place pedagogies is also transformative: 'Although some non-Indigenous educators may initially be reticent and skeptical about embracing critical, place-based understandings of Indigenous epistemologies and ontologies, with gentle encouragement and skillful facilitation, such approaches can prove deeply transformative for all' (Lowan-Trudeau, 2018: 524). An anti-racist approach to PBL recognises core issues at the heart of settler relationships with place, including 'the actual question of belonging in a place where one's history is short, and which one occupies as the inheritor of violence'; globalisation and place; and embodied ecological connectivity, which requires 'settlers to acknowledge our connections with indigenous peoples and with nature' (Bird Rose & Robin, 2004: n.p.).

We cannot fully engage in PBL without authentic reflection on how our notions of place are entangled with legacies of racism and without consideration of Indigenous knowledges and histories of the place/s we are teaching in and with. In advocating for a pedagogy that aims to develop a learner's environmental responsibility, we must also recognise that such ambitious goals cannot be achieved in isolation and must intersect with other social justice imperatives, including anti-racist pedagogy and its movement towards anti-racist Shakespeare.

Towards a Conceptual Framework for Teaching Place-Based Shakespeare

The seven core concepts described in this section are fundamental to understanding how PBL supports the teaching of Shakespeare. They also underpin the model (Figure 13) and practical activities in Section 4.

1. PBL highlights the stories of place

O pardon, since a crooked figure may
Attest in little place a million,
And let us, ciphers to this great account,
On your imaginary forces work. (*Henry V*, Prologue 15–18)

In the prologue to *Henry V*, the Chorus imagines the limited space of the playhouse cramming into its 'wooden O' so 'great an object' as 'the vasty fields of France' (11–13). One actor on the stage takes the 'place' of a million. The place of the play is constructed through storytelling, imagination and the interaction between the material physical environment and representational discourse. Shakespeare's Chorus gives us our first lesson for a place-based framework: the constitutive role of stories in making place.

Place is constituted by stories: stories make place, places generate stories. As such, place is never one thing; one place is 'a million' places. As a palimpsestic multi-storied phenomenon, we must approach place with respect for its diversity of stories. We should look for stories rendered invisible or marginalised; more-than-human stories; a learner's personal stories; the stories we create and imagine; and the stories we learn and experience in place (including the relationship between the texts we study and the places we study in).

2. PBL understands place as a complex, open-ended phenomenon

> What beast was't then
> That made you break this enterprise to me?
> When you durst do it, then you were a man;
> And to be more than what you were, you would
> Be so much more the man. Nor time nor place
> Did then adhere, and yet you would make both:
> They have made themselves, and that their fitness now
> Does unmake you. (*Macbeth*, 1.7.47–54)

Place is a complex phenomenon, personified by Lady Macbeth as self-making. She suggests that place is shifting, dynamic and changeable; the place has 'made' itself fit for purpose 'now', but this manifestation of place is transient. Because place is complex, it cannot be controlled and the interactions a learner has with it cannot be predicted. It is produced through interactions, and thus the way educators and learners engage with place during a Shakespeare lesson will impact not only the teaching of Shakespeare but the place itself. The 'making' of place is ongoing and will change through the interactions between educator, learner, text and place.

3. Place is subjective in PBL

> Come on, sir, here's the place. Stand still: how fearful
> And dizzy 'tis to cast one's eyes so low.
> The crows and choughs that wing the midway air
> Show scarce so gross as beetles. (*King Lear*, 4.6.11–14)

The specific place experienced by an individual is idiosyncratic yet essential for place-based work. In *King Lear*, Edgar leads his blind, tormented father to what he describes as a cliff's edge, duping him into believing he can fall and end his life. This place is experienced entirely differently by the characters within it; for the blind Gloucester, it is produced through discourse and interaction with his disguised son. Gloucester and Edgar are in the same fictional place, but they have divergent place-based experiences. Without respecting and acknowledging the potential for place to produce diverse experiences, we cannot effectively implement PBL.

4. PBL sees multiple dimensions of place

Generated by the subjectivity of place is its multiplicity. In *All's Well That Ends Well*, the ailing King laments his situation; infirm and elderly, he feels that he occupies a space he no longer merits: 'I fill a place, I know't' (1.2.69), and

> Since I nor wax nor honey can bring home,
> I quickly were dissolved from my hive
> To give some laborers room. (1.2.65–67)

Place here takes on multiple meanings: metaphorical, symbolic and literal. His occupation of the throne is physical and political, and his concern is rooted in the embodied experience of ageing. He uses the metaphorical, more-than-human place of the beehive to explain his feeling out of place, unable to contribute and taking up 'room'. The 'place' of the King brings into play multiple dimensions and is seen through different lenses: hierarchical political place, physical embodiment and ageing, more-than-human and spatial metaphors.

Learners should undertake place-based work through different, interdisciplinary dimensions, lenses or frames (from political to ecological, economic to aesthetic) to deepen their understanding of the multiplicity of place.

5. In PBL, place is connected

Ay, now am I in Arden, the more fool I! When I was at home I was in a better place, but travellers must be content. (*As You Like It*, 2.4.14–16)

Touchstone reflects on one place by comparison with another: 'Arden' against the 'better place' of 'home'. In this, he demonstrates that place is never understood in isolation but rather through its connections to other places. Places are created and connected through dynamic webs of relation, as Beames advocates in the final step of his PBL framework, critical cosmopolitanism, where students recognise how places are interconnected (2015: 29). Place-based learning encourages the development of our ability to discern and generate connections across places (including lived and literary senses of place) to deepen understanding.

6. PBL promotes responsibility to place

'Have you forgot all sense of place and duty?' (*Othello*, 2.3.163)

In chastising Cassio and Montano's inappropriate behaviour, Iago espouses a belief that actions must fit the time and place. It is our responsibility to behave in certain ways depending on the place in which we are embedded; we have a duty to place. While Iago means a professional, social and class obligation, this can also be a prompt to think about our responsibilities to place. What is our 'sense of place', and have we forgotten our duty to it?

Place-based education has an activist agenda, with sustainability, climate change mitigation and environmental awareness core tenets of its approach. For many place-based scholars, the aim is to deepen not only a learner's knowledge of place but their respect for place. Place-based learning is about more than learning to satisfy course requirements; it must be driven by broader goals around environmental sustainability, community growth and individual self-development.

And if a Shakespeare class can produce critical thinking and stimulate attention to environmental or sociopolitical issues that matter to our students, then PBL can help to assert the relevance and urgency of literary studies.

7. In PBL, place can be both the topic and the teacher

The very place puts toys of desperation
Without more motive into every brain
That looks so many fathoms to the sea
And hears it roar beneath. (*Hamlet*, 1.4.75–78)

Place has power and agency, as Horatio attempts to persuade Hamlet (in the Second Quarto (Q2)). In PBL, place is a partner or agent in the learning process. Far less ominously than Horatio implies here, place may engage us and our learners in ways that can teach us, developing new knowledge and ways of knowing.

REFLECTION IN PLACE

For this 'Reflection in Place', I invite you to consider:

- Where would you position your practice and philosophy on a continuum of place-responsiveness?
- How might anti-racist Shakespeare pedagogy intersect with your sense of place?
- What might be a 'small change' you could make to your place-based teaching and learning?

Embracing the complex phenomenon of place presents challenges to educators in a high-stakes, highly regulated educational environment.

It also holds rich, exciting potential to invigorate our teaching of Shakespeare, fostering urgency and relevance, stimulating engagement and interest, and supporting learning that develops not only a student's knowledge of Shakespeare's works but a critical awareness of and investment in the places in which they live, and which they will help to shape during the course of their education and beyond.

2 Defining Place: Lived and Literary Place in the Shakespeare Classroom

In 2018, I ran a professional development seminar on *Macbeth* and place for secondary school teachers working in Townsville, North Queensland. I was only beginning to explore how place might be integrated into Shakespeare classrooms. I asked the participants what sense of place their students had. It quickly became evident that teachers felt concerned about their pupils' limited knowledge of local place. Several teachers mentioned that their students had never visited an area of Townsville known as 'The Strand', a photogenic, popular beachside promenade. Participants felt their students lacked understanding of or engagement with place. Students, teachers suspected, were hyperlocal and familiar with direct, immediate locations like bus routes, bedrooms and schools. But if students are not familiar with landmarks deemed significant by local culture, what relationship might they have to foreign, exotic, historical or invented places like the Scotland of *Macbeth* or the playing houses of early modern London? Before we practice place-based Shakespeare, we need to reflect on the meaning of place for educators and for learners.

If you were asked to define place, you might find it paradoxically self-explanatory and impossible to define.[10] We cannot do without place.

---

[10] Things would become even more complicated if we considered terms like space, ecology, the environment, nature, country, landscape, wilderness, urban, regional or rural place. For a discussion of the vexed question of place versus space, see Cresswell (2015), Casey (1997, 2009), Pawlicka-Deger (2021: 322) and Mayne (2009: 176). For a theoretical problematisation of nature, see Morton (2010). For a definition of the rural, see Corbett and Donehower (2017).

It shapes our identities, and yet (or perhaps because of this) we find it very difficult to conceptualise. Casey writes:

> To be at all – to exist in any way – is to be somewhere, and to be somewhere is to be in some kind of place. Place is as requisite as the air we breathe, the ground on which we stand, the bodies we have. We are surrounded by places. We walk over and through them. We live in places, relate to others in them, die in them. Nothing we do is unplaced. How could it be otherwise? How could we fail to recognize this primal fact? (1997: 9)

We rarely accord place the importance it warrants (Casey, 2009: xiii) in terms of its shaping influence on our lives and learning. While 'nothing we do is unplaced', place is not a concrete concept. In the 1970s, Edward Relph identified a 'real problem' with a lack of knowledge around place (1976: 6). Tim Cresswell observes that 'there has been very little considered under-standing of what the word "place" means', perhaps because it 'seems to speak for itself' (2015: 1). Given its ubiquity, 'it is a problem that no one quite knows what they are talking about when they are talking about place' (2015: 6). There is 'no such thing as a quickly representable meaning of place' (Nakagawa & Payne, 2017: 158). Place has 'no singular unique identity' (Wattchow & Brown, 2011: 101). It is a 'nebulous concept' (Orr, 1992: 126), simple, complicated and 'contested' (Cresswell, 2015: 18). Potter calls it 'a dappled construction, shifting always in and out of the light' (2009: 72–3). It will always be 'an elusive conceptual construct' whose meanings are 'never stable' (Wattchow & Brown, 2011: 87). From a PBL perspective, this is problematic, because to engage place pedagogically, 'one must first explore its meanings' (Gruenewald, 2003b: 622).

Section 2 of *Shakespeare and Place-Based Learning* aims to explore its meanings by examining how learners perceive and respond to place in Shakespeare classrooms. Over four years, tertiary students studying Shakespeare in English units at James Cook University (JCU) were asked to reflect on how they interpreted the concept of place and its relationship to their learning. Survey respondents predominantly comprised

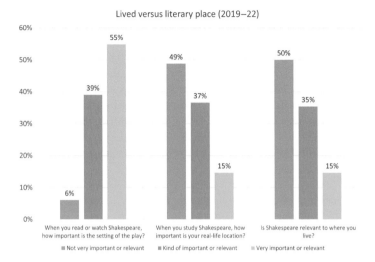

Figure 1 James Cook University (JCU) survey response data (June 2019 to June 2022) (n=82).

Bachelor of Arts and Bachelor of Education students studying Shakespeare as part of undergraduate coursework between 2019 and 2022. Students were asked to rate the importance and relevance of lived (real life) and literary place (setting) to their study of Shakespeare's plays (Figure 1). They were also asked to explain their rating.[11] Students were not given a definition of place. Their responses, like the definitions canvassed here, indicate conflicting, diverse understandings of not only place but also Shakespeare and identity.

The results demonstrate a stark contrast between the value students ascribe to lived and literary place. While 55 per cent of students believed setting to be 'very important or relevant', only 15 per cent of students

---

[11] Survey responses were anonymous. They are coded by order of submission and referred to numerically.

believed their real-life location to be very important to their study of Shakespeare. This raises a problematic question: how do students engage with fictional places and settings if their own lived experiences of place are devalued?

The eighty-two responses received over the period 2019–22 were coded thematically into broad categories, with each response assigned 1–3 categories (Table 1).[12] Four key threads were prominent: the influence of regionality on students' thinking about place; a marked and often conscious separation between literary place and a student's sense of place; the social construction of place; and diverse, conflicting definitions of place itself.

'Not a Lot of Room for Shakespeare': The Influence of Regionality and the Need to Reimagine the Regions

One of the dominant themes in student responses was the self-conscious awareness of the students' embeddedness in a 'regional' location.[13] Most of these students lived in Townsville and surrounding areas of North Queensland. Townsville's population of 234,000 people includes an Indigenous population more than twice the national average (9 per cent versus 3.2 per cent nationwide) and a tertiary education level under the national average (16.4 per cent of Townsville residents have a bachelor's degree or higher, compared with a national average of 26.3 per cent).[14] The city is regional in relation to metropolitan centres: it is approximately 15 hours' drive north of Queensland's capital city, Brisbane. But like many facets of place, regionality is highly subjective: to a student living in Wilton or Charters Towers, Townsville represents a bigger urban centre. To a student living in Brisbane, Sydney or Melbourne, Townsville will feel 'regional'. The description of Townsville I have just painted demonstrates

---

[12] Blank or outlier responses were excluded. In 2019, a second survey was conducted because of a technical glitch in the first survey. Quantitative data from the first survey was excluded.

[13] See Massey (1994) for problems with the concept of 'regionality'. The words 'regional' and 'rural' were not used in the survey questions.

[14] Australian Bureau of Statistics, 'Townsville', 2021 Census All Persons QuickStats, https://abs.gov.au/census/find-census-data/quickstats/2021/318.

Table 1 Codes from James Cook University (JCU) student surveys (2019–22).

Codes	Code Description	Count
Physical environment	References to materials or features that the learner needed in their physical environment to engage with Shakespeare.	12
Irrelevant	Indicated that place was irrelevant to the study of Shakespeare.	35
Relevant	Indicated links between their place and Shakespeare.	22
Fictional setting	Reference to the fictional setting of the play/s.	14
Adaptation	Reference to modernisations or adaptations of Shakespeare.	7
Rural	Defined their place as rural, regional or remote.	13
Theme	Reference to Shakespeare's themes, issues, messages, plot, historical context.	15
Universality	Reference to Shakespeare as 'universal'.	9
Family[*]	Defined place as family or personal interactions.	5
Education/ profession	Reference to place in terms of their education or future teaching profession.	7

[*] This code was also identified in another recent study (Bass et al., 2020).

exactly what Michael Corbett articulates in his discussion of the rural: 'We desperately attempt to finally know the physical reality of the rural by measuring distances (usually from urban areas), population densities and by alluding to productive activities and landscapes' (2013: 2).[15] Townsville, like any place, is not just one thing, and its regionality is not fixed. We see this clearly in one outlier response, from respondent 47, that contradicted the pattern of student responses:

> Townsville is full of Shakespearean drama. High crime, inequality, obvious military presence, political power junkies, all in a beautiful setting with free exercise equipment lining well maintained parks with friendly wildlife cheering families and athletes as they share this multicultural space. (47)

This student generates a starkly different Townsville to the city as depicted in news media or statistics.

The concept of the region is undoubtedly vexed, but the influence of regionality on student self-identification speaks to the importance of a 'critically regional Shakespeare' and 'thinking regionally' when it comes to Shakespeare studies (Greenberg, 2019: 341). For some students, as we see in the responses that follow, this significantly influenced their understanding of the relationship between lived place and their study of Shakespeare.

> Shakespeare isn't important in Townsville. I think its not valued in our society. (26)
>
> Being from Townsville, which could be considered as uncultured, I don't feel Shakespeare is very important. (18)
>
> Townsville is not exactly a city of culture. (50)
>
> Shakespeare is part of almost every English speaker's learning so I don't think where you are would affect if you read it or not. The same can be said for enjoying his plays, even someone in rural areas may enjoy his works. (3)

---

[15] For more on a critical approach to reading 'regionality', see Hansen (2019: 4–5).

> I live in a rural area. There is not [a lot] of room for Shakespeare – though given small town conflicts you would see his plots acted out in real life. (37)

> I live in a small town [Mackay] so kinda of irrelevant, my town is focused on real world issues and doesn't really care for literature (67)

> I don't see, nor have I been able to find the value that Shakespeare holds as someone who lives in FNQ [Far North Queensland]. Perhaps if I was wealthy and without a care in the world I could enjoy the whimsical nature of stories like MnightsDream which could benefit in a tropical setting. But what I need are stories of humanity that I can relate to and even see reflected in the environment I live on, such as politically or domestically. (58)

> I live in a regional area where the topic of Shakespeare is limited to a small group of people or mainly senior English students who had to take the subject. (42)

> We live in a really rural town, the only exposure to this kind of literature is in school or in cities an hour and a half away (78)

These responses align with what Demarest calls an 'inner script' related to how learners perceive their place (2015: 132). Many of these students prefaced their response by explaining that they are 'from Townsville' or 'live in a regional area' or 'a really rural town'. They intend this to be self-explanatory: these labels of regionality and rurality are anathema to valuing Shakespeare. There is a clear gap, in these students' minds, between Shakespeare and regional Australia. This gap intersects place with class and socioeconomic status. Respondents understand these terms (rural, regional, FNQ) to connote more than geographical location. They have 'internalized the notion', common in rural areas, 'that their place isn't important enough to matter' (Ball & Lai, 2006: 272). The implication in these responses situates rural places 'as problematic deficit spaces' (Corbett & Donehower, 2017: 9; Walker-Gibbs, 2013: 128). This suggests students are not engaging directly with their place in these responses but rather their sense of place is 'mediated and distorted' by stereotypes (Wattchow & Brown, 2011: 96). This adoption of assumed external perspectives on regional place is seen in respondent 18's use of the passive voice in their statement that Townsville 'could be considered as uncultured'. Respondent 3's qualification that 'even someone in rural areas' may enjoy Shakespeare illustrates that they have a preconceived idea that lived place influences one's engagement with Shakespeare. This is extended by respondents 42 and 78, who indicate that Shakespeare belongs to only niche subsections of place. Respondent 37 reveals slippage between the physicality of the student's reference to place – 'a rural area', a 'small town' – and the conceptual space they occupy, which does not have a lot of cultural 'room' for Shakespeare (although there is something subversive in the appropriation of Shakespearean plots to characterise local behaviour). From these student perspectives, 'Shakespeare appears to be a good way from necessity', and those who do engage with Shakespeare in these places 'mark themselves' as educated people (Corbett, 2013: 4).

Perceived interpretation of place appears to be more powerful than the students' own experiences, with the former prioritised over the latter. In thinking about place, learners fall back on 'cultural templates' that are 'persistent and pervasive'. These internalised values and ideas 'diminish the potential of local places' (Wattchow & Brown, 2011: 95). The privileging of perceived beliefs about place over lived, personal experience indicates that students do not believe they have agency in determining what constitutes place. Crucially, the students' awareness of the stigmatisation of regional Far North Queensland directly affects their evaluation of the 'importance' of studying Shakespeare. These responses reinforce that, in PBL, focusing on a student's 'local' context can be problematic (Ball & Lai, 2006: 268). While many PBL scholars and practitioners prioritise the local (Gruenewald & Smith, 2014b: xiii; Ball & Lai, 2006: 262, 282; Demarest, 2015: 1; Smith, 2002: 586), there are limits and challenges to its pedagogical use.[16] 'Just because something is "local" (in the sense of being physically proximate) does not necessarily mean that it will always be particularly

---

[16] For exceptions, see Kenway (2009), McInerney et al. (2011: 10) and Green and Clark (2013).

familiar or meaningful to students' (Ball & Lai, 2006: 268). While some learners may be 'sufficiently interested in their place', others may have 'internalized the notion that their place isn't important enough to matter' (Ball & Lai, 2006: 272), assume the stories of some places are 'better' than others (Demarest, 2015: 129), find visits to local place 'contrived' (Loh, 2018: n.p.), express indifference to the local or be resistant to critical pedagogy's 'emphasis on the politics of socioecological transformation' (Ball & Lai, 2006: 262). A sole focus on the local might constrain student learning (Beames, 2015: 28) or entrench traditional power relations (Cameron, 2014: 294). More troublingly, using the local can be problematic because some learners may feel alienated from local place due to oppression, marginalisation or exclusion (Gannon, 2009b: 608; Corbett, 2013: 1). 'Why would students want to engage in learning that seeks to nurture a love of a place where they feel excluded or oppressed?' (McInerney et al., 2011: 10). This aligns with Dadabhoy and Mehdizadeh's warning that teaching Shakespeare as 'universal' can be harmful (2023: 12). The assumption that local place is universally relevant and meaningful can be equally damaging. Place 'cannot be uncritically assumed or dogmatically imposed in pedagogies' (Nakagawa & Payne, 2017: 147). Throughout the student responses, assumptions about regional North Queensland and Shakespeare's place*less*ness there are pervasive. This demonstrates that perception of one's local place and its perceived significance impacts the value of Shakespeare for people in that location.

This is strong evidence of the need for a reimagining of place (Gannon, 2009b: 614; Walker-Gibbs, 2013: 127). The students' perceived disconnection between regional Queensland and Shakespeare resonates with an important question asked by Gannon in her work on place-based pedagogies in western Sydney: 'How do young people feel about, take up, or resist the stigmatization of the places they call home?' (2009b: 608). Resistance and reimagining are needed not only to reclaim the identities of students' local regional place but to reclaim their right to engage with literary and dramatic texts (like Shakespeare's) in those places. The responses drawn from this survey indicate a need for site-specific projects like Gannon's, which enable students 'living in a place marked by deficit discourses' to take up 'discursive space' and 'begin to tell it otherwise' (2009b: 621). In this way, 'place-based pedagogies are timely and important' (2009b: 622). Imagine the potential if these learners felt that their place enabled, rather than repressed, their engagement with Shakespeare. A belief that Shakespeare's texts belong in and are valued within a learner's sense of place is a gift for the educator. A learner is more likely to feel capable of engaging with the text if they believe there is 'room' for Shakespeare.

'Of Little Importance': Separating Literary Place and Lived Place

Sense of place can at times be paradoxical. While many respondents believed that their regionality negatively impacted the relevance of Shakespeare, they also expressed a belief that their lived sense of place had no impact on their study of Shakespeare. Responses in the 'irrelevant' category (Table 1) included comments such as: 'I don't find where I am relevant to me enjoying or understanding his works' (102); 'Where I live, work, or study has no bearing on my engagement with the plays' (88); 'I don't see an immediate connection with my everyday environment and Shakespeare' (84); 'I consider my real-life location quite irrelevant to my study' (83); 'I don't see any relationship' (82); 'my own real life location has no bearing on my study of Shakespeare' (74); 'I don't think my real life location matters' (54); 'it seems of little importance' (55); 'it doesn't resonate with the world that I see daily' (58). The vehemence of these responses might prove intimidating for an educator seeking to implement place-based approaches to teaching Shakespeare.

Not only was place articulated as irrelevant but several students expressed a belief that it was the learner's responsibility to actively repress any connection between lived and literary place.

> I have to separate where I live to studying the texts in some way so that I can fully immerse myself in Shakespeare's created world. However, using Shakespeare as a reference for studying human emotions and behaviour means that I cannot wholly separate myself from the world I live in. Shakespeare's satirical observations can be easily applied to modern politics, societal convention, and even humour. (12)

I tend to focus on the world that Shakespeare was trying to create rather than trying to associate it with myself and where I live. (62)

Where the scene is set is important to understand the true meaning behind the lines. Whilst where I am at the moment isn't necessarily important as it's the play we are concentrating on. Since i study and am a reader in general i love Shakespeare and all the hidden meanings behind words and phrases. (8)

For these students, the appropriate way to engage with Shakespeare requires 'concentrating' on the play and isolating that experience from 'where I am at the moment'. Responsible engagement with Shakespeare incorporates a dissociation from their immediate place, which is an unnecessary distraction from the 'immersive' experience of finding Shakespeare's 'hidden meanings'. The value of Shakespeare is understood as more important than connecting Shakespeare to the students' experience. Yet, despite advocating separation from their place to support immersion in Shakespeare, respondent 12 simultaneously notes an inability to 'wholly separate myself from the world I live in' because of the ease with which Shakespeare can be 'applied' to the student's contemporary sociopolitical context. Like respondent 12, respondent 83 evokes a tension between a disavowal and recognition of the influence of place:

I consider my real-life location quite irrelevant to my study. Though it influences my life and experiences, which in turn affects my interpretations, the universal themes of Shakespeare make my exact location quite unimportant. . . . I marked Shakespeare as somewhat important to where I live as – again – his work is universally relevant. However, I wouldn't say it is specifically significant to where I live. (83)

Despite claiming that their location is 'irrelevant', students 12 and 83 simultaneously provide justification for why their lived experience *does* matter, because it 'affects my interpretations'. However, Shakespeare's 'universality' – what Chris Thurman refers to as 'that multivalent, contested word' (2014: 11) – undermines the value of the respondent's 'exact location'. Discourses around Shakespeare are invoked as a way of minimising and marginalising the value of the learner's place: universality trumps locality.

Students are well-trained at identifying what is and is not relevant to their learning. Respondent 50 identified 'themes and messages' as the 'important parts of Shakespeare ... not the "set dressing"', confirming that setting is commonly seen as 'a subordinate albeit necessary consideration' (Green & Clark, 2013: 3). As Semler astutely observes, 'Our system determines that which it is relevant for us to embrace and when' (2013: 87). Learners know how the system works; SysEd has no time for place, and so nor do they. In fact, it might actively inhibit their 'immersion' and 'concentration' (Respondents 12 and 8). These students are performing 'good studentship', which occurs within what Semler calls a 'band of perceived relevance' (2013: 89).

> The 'band of perceived relevance' refers to the internalised, subject-specific protocols that govern normally acceptable discourse in class within any discipline. Obedient system creatures, be they students or teachers, remain within the band of perceived relevance in what they say, think and do in class or in a course of study. They are good system creatures functioning in obedience to SysEd and furthering its ends by their compliant teaching and learning. When an educator breaks the band of perceived relevance by overtly driving the classroom discourse in a direction contrary to that which is tacitly and explicitly considered relevant it puts a strain on the social situation, yet it has the virtue of highlighting the limits of thought imposed by the band and opens the possibility of fresh discoveries beyond it. (Semler, 2016: 7)

Simply asking students to think about place in relation to Shakespeare through these surveys caused disruption to SysEd – and we have not even begun to implement place-based Shakespeare yet. Place thus offers both 'fresh discoveries' and sticky challenges. Students obedient to SysEd may, in Semler's words, 'ferociously resist alternative approaches' foisted on them by educators (2016: 7), as we see in some of the student responses. Place-based Shakespeare troubles the waters of SysEd, and it requires a rethinking of relevance, engagement and learning. As Semler writes, when relevance expands, learning seems to point 'inward as well as outward' (2013: 104). To teach Shakespeare with place is to ask students to engage in two challenging cognitive and emotional processes: to reflect on their own sense of place and to reconsider the structure of the educational systems they inhabit.

'We Shape Our Own Spaces': Social Space and Shakespeare

For a small but significant percentage of respondents (Table 1; approximately 6 per cent), place was understood not as a geographical location but as a site of social interactions and familial relationships. Respondent 17 wrote:

> As Shakespeare's work is about people and their social circumstances, the social setting is very important. People have not changed, in my opinion. This may explain how Shakespeare's work is still relevant. I live outside of town because I like to have people at arm's length. I am however, fascinated [by] how people negotiate social expectations. Shakespeare spotlights this and makes us all look closer at how we shape our own spaces. (17)

Here, physical location (living 'outside of town') is interwoven with social behaviours (keeping people at 'arm's length') and social interactions ('negotiating' social expectations). Shakespeare 'spotlights' respondent 17's social setting and the ways in which 'we shape our own spaces', which implies that Shakespeare helps to illuminate the social construction of place.

Other respondents interpreted the question of the relationship between Shakespeare and place as a question about family.

My family doesn't really care about shakespeare, but I do enjoy some of his works personally. (27)

I have always enjoyed Shakespeare as my Grandma has always been a theatre enthusiast and took me to see the plays when I was young (6)

My home has no relevance to Shakespeare, we do not have many Shakespeare texts in the house (59)

Having studied Romeo & Juliet in highschool I found that place was very relevant (being from a small town with a lot of family dramas). Currently I am studying As You Like It and have found place rather removed from my current place. (95)

[M]y family have not been interested in Shakespear, I only know of him and his plays through school (primary and high school), however I did not know of him until I moved to Australia. (73)

For these students, place is constituted by familial interactions and the 'home'. These respondents reaffirm what place-based scholars have also identified: relationships and family members influence the experience of place (Gannon, 2009b: 616; Wyse et al., 2012: 1028–9). Place is a social, relational construction generated by 'connections' (Corbett, 2013: 2) and networks of social relations (Massey, 1994: 5). Predominantly, though, these relational constructions of place exclude Shakespeare. If Shakespeare's works help us to look closer at how we 'shape our own spaces' (17), then the belief that Shakespeare does not belong in place limits opportunities to engage with Shakespeare and to critically reflect on place. These responses indicate the relational nature of place and that this sense of place can influence a learner's engagement with Shakespeare. While some respondents felt that a 'sense of place' did not belong in the Shakespeare classroom, others felt that Shakespeare did not belong in their relational or social place. In different ways, respondents indicated a clear disconnect between their perceptions of Shakespeare education and their sense of place.

'We Share a Certain Similarity': Disparate Interpretations
of Place

The responses canvassed here reinforce that, as Doreen Massey writes, 'The identities of place are always unfixed, contested and multiple' (1994: 5). Some respondents interpreted place in reference to their regionality, family dynamics or their home. Some responded by discussing their physical environment and environmental factors like a 'quiet' location for their study of Shakespeare (107). In contrast to this hyperlocalised interpretation, other respondents interpreted place as a broad reference to their 'modern day era' (41) or in relation to themes: 'I think that Shakespeare is sometimes relevant to where I live due to dominant themes such as love, hate, jealousy, pain, betrayal etc. It occurs where I live. Time wise and area wise' (68). Others saw place as globalised and non-specific: 'Shakespeare is relevant to every place – ideas and themes that transpose across many cultures and places' (19). Only two respondents made an explicit connection between their place and the study of a specific play:

> I live in an area close to an abundance of different flora and fauna. There are houses built but not all of them are fully done and they sit just right outside of the entrance to some really dense bush land area. Like the court and Arden I feel as though we share a certain similarity. (15)
>
> My own setting shapes and influences my own experiences and values, which I bring to my readings. While Cairns is a far, far cry from 16th Century England, Shakespeare is relevant in many ways. While we enjoy many liberties, we are still faced with gender issues, identity issues, we romanticise escaping the pressures within our own lives to somewhere more simple and beautiful. Additionally, we are currently experiencing more government controls and an absence of art, dictated by Covid restrictions. Finally, with a high homelessness rate in Cairns, as in Shakespeare's works and times, class is very much an issue. (72)

Respondent 15's shared spatial 'similarity' between the pastoral and court settings of *As You Like It* with local bushland and new developments generates a personal connection between literary and lived place. This response offers a fleeting glimpse of learner-generated PBL. Here, the respondent reflected on development and environmental sustainability through their knowledge of Shakespeare's settings in *As You Like It* and, conversely, used their local knowledge of place to better understand the play's settings. Respondent 72 also implicitly drew on *As You Like It* to make explicit links between their sense of place and Shakespeare, using the play's interests in the pastoral, exile, identity, gender and class to critically reflect on sociocultural issues in twenty-first-century Cairns. These students exhibited potential for 'place essential' PBL at the advanced end of the place-responsiveness continuum (Beames, 2015; see Section 1). They listened to the stories of place, articulated a personal sense of place and were able to bring Shakespeare's *As You Like It* and their individual places into productive, mutually illuminating dialogue.

A Definition of Place

Place was defined by the respondents in diverse ways, through exclusions, comparisons, experiences, interactions and sociopolitical and ideological discourses. To account for this, we need a complexivist perspective that understands place as composed of interacting parts which dynamically form and reform. My definition of place, while designed for Shakespeare educators, is applicable to any literary studies pedagogies. This definition comprises what I refer to as 'dimensions' and 'modes' of place, which underpin the model of place-based Shakespeare in Section 4.

Dimensions of Place

A dimension of place is one manifestation or form of place. A sense of place is formed through the interaction of multiple dimensions, which generates further dimensions of place. In Shakespeare classrooms, dimensions of place beyond the three canvassed here – setting, material and imagined place – could include virtual place (see Section 4), Indigenous Country (itself a complex interaction of land, culture, community, history and spirituality), theatrical place and more-than-human place.

Setting. In literary studies pedagogy, the concept of setting is central to thinking about place. This 'deceptively simple' literary construct refers to the where and when of a story (Wyse, 2021: 13), its location, historical and social context (Klarer, 2011: 33, 191). Setting is often taken for granted or disconnected from 'how students perceive their own surroundings' (Wyse, 2021: 13–14; Demarest, 2015: 63). Although 94 per cent of students surveyed indicated that fictional settings were somewhat or very important to the study of Shakespeare, very few articulated *why* or provided examples. In contrast, their discussions of their lived place (even in disavowing that place's importance) were often animated and detailed. This suggests that the importance attributed to fictional setting over lived place is often a reflection of 'espoused theories' (Argyris & Schön, 1974: 6–7) rather than a genuine belief, just as the devaluation of lived place indicates a similar espousal of perceived values at play. In place-based Shakespeare, setting or the fictional playworld may comprise historical, imagined, material and theatrical dimensions. Setting is a critical agent in the construction of place, establishing a major dynamic between literary place and a student's lived experience of place. This tension is central to place-based Shakespeare.

Material place. In its simplest form, place is a physical or environmental location, defined by 'natural features or scientific concepts' or by regional, political or natural boundaries (Demarest, 2015: 72). We understand place on a human scale by dividing place into concepts like a household, a community or forty acres (Orr, 1992: 126). This is the place we can see, touch or border. Material place also encompasses more-than-human place; it moves well beyond a sense of place as constructed by or in service to humans. Material place generates productive tension with setting and imagined place.

Imagined place. The production of place involves imaginative work that implicates histories and memories. An individual's 'capacity to form internal images or ideas of objects and situations not actually present to the senses' will shape how we interact with and construct place.[17] The act of relating to place itself occurs within what Greenwood calls 'imagined place', where the human psyche colours our experiences and ensures that we only come to know places

---

[17] 'Imagination, n.', *OED Online*, Oxford University Press, December 2022.

'as our imagined experience of them' (Greenwood, 2019: 368). The role of the imagination in constructing, understanding and experiencing place is well-documented (Green & Clark, 2013: 8; Wattchow & Brown, 2011: 20; Kenway, 2009: 201, 203). As the imagination can be understood as 'mentally combining' sensory data and images of qualities, objects and situations we have previously experienced,[18] place is inevitably a product of our imaginations, histories and memories. When we engage with the histories of a particular site, consider the climate or conditions of a location or think about past or future engagements with place, we inevitably do imaginative work to construct our sense of that place, our relationship with it and its entanglements with other agents. Imagination is thus integral to the shaping of our experience of place both within literary studies and beyond.

Modes of Place

Place is not only defined by its dimensions; it is also defined by styles or modes of interaction which continually generate phenomena of place. I identify three modes of place in Shakespeare pedagogy: place as an event, the social or relational construction of place and place as an epistemological process. Like my dimensions of place, these are not exhaustive, and further modes of place could include a substantialist mode, which approaches place as an object rather than a process.

The eventmentality of place. Place is not a 'thing' but a 'process' (Casey, 1997: 337). It can be understood as an event; 'things happen *in it*, but *it happens too* – it has its own historicity, its own eventmentality' (Casey, 2009: xxv, emphasis in original). This relational perspective contrasts the more traditional substantialist mode and moves away from place-as-object to place-as-process (McInerney et al., 2011: 9; Cresswell, 2015: 71; Massey, 2005: 13). If place is understood as an event, it loses its status as static, disconnected background and becomes an affective agent in the action of learning. In thinking of place as an event, we foreground the complexivist view that place is constituted by human and more-than-human interactions, which aligns with the relational mode of place.

---

[18] Ibid.

Relational place. Scholarship on place – in philosophy, cultural geography, place studies – has persuasively recognised that the concept is at least partially socially constructed (Gruenewald, 2014: 143–4; Massey, 1994: 22; Cresswell, 2015: 46–51).[19] This transforms the way we think about place from something static and bounded to 'open and porous networks of social relations' (Massey, 1994: 121). In this view, a place's identities are generated through interactions and continually under development (Massey, 1994: 121; 2005: 9). This makes place complex, because any one place can be constructed and interpreted differently, so that a single place holds multiple identities (Relph, 1976: 56). While useful, the recognition of place as socially constructed is limited by its anthropocentrism and countered by claims that place has inherent meaning (Wattchow & Brown, 2011: 89; Relph, 1976: 47–8) and that society itself is a product of place (Cresswell, 2015: 49). A better term for the complex construction of place is to recognise that it is 'relationally constituted'. This recognises 'complex, more than material, and more than human forces, in the ongoing constitution of place' (Potter & Magner, 2018: 1). This expansive framing of place as

[19] This emphasis on the social construction of place raises 'one of the most fundamental problems' for scholars of place: is place constructed through human experience or does place have its own inherent meaning to be discovered by those who engage with it? (Wattchow & Brown, 2011: 87). The social construction of place has been critiqued by scholars, as Casey reviews (2009: 46–51). This claim may seem 'heretical' to those with an 'ecocentric view', as socially constructed place might seem 'the ultimate expression of anthropocentric hubris'. However, Gruenewald explains that this term relates to the acknowledgement that 'people and cultures' invest places with meaning (2003b: 626). He adds that 'acknowledging that places are social constructions does not negate the idea that places such as ecosystems, trees, and wilderness have other qualities that transcend the often place-destructive purposes of human beings. It simply allows that human beings are responsible for place making' (2003b: 626). For Gruenewald, it is vital to recognise that places are 'products of human decisions' and should be thought of critically (2003b: 627). Other place theorists have also identified frameworks for defining place that hinge on its social construction. Pawlicka-Deger builds on Henri Lefebvre's 'three ways of interweaving society with space' (2021: 322–3). Cresswell uses John A. Agnew's three fundamental aspects of place (2015: 12–14).

relational acknowledges that place emerges through complex interactions between and among humans and more-than-humans.

Place as a way of knowing. Place is also an epistemological mode. Andrew Bozio, in his work on early modern theatrical place, argues that place and cognition are co-constructed: place is constructed through cognition, and cognition is aided by the environment. From a cognitive ecology perspective, early modern thinking was 'an environmental phenomenon' (Bozio, 2020: 9). Place thus helps us to think; as an epistemological process, it offers 'a way of seeing, knowing, and understanding the world' (Cresswell, 2015: 18). In this way, place is also pedagogical (Gruenewald, 2003b: 621).[20] For PBL, this mode of place is critical: recognising the interplay between place and knowing helps us to position place as an agent in the learning process. This mode of knowing may also be embodied, following Somerville's PBL framework.

Sense of Place

The interaction of some or all of these dimensions and modes of place generates an individual's 'sense of place'. This nebulous phrase incorporates an individual's perception of their environments.[21] It can be considered as a phenomenon emerging from the interaction of the facets of place described in this definition of place, while also being more than the sum of its parts. It relies on material place, our imaginative work, relational constructions, knowledge and interactions. Sense of place emphasises the 'subjective dimensions of place' (Prieto, 2011: 15) and can be understood as a 'constructed reality' comprising a learner's unique experiences, memories and histories (Azano, 2011: 1). Mundell argues that it contains three components: the creation of a text, the product and the reader's interpretation (2018: 3). It is vital for place-based educators to recognise the complexity and diversity of our learners' sense of place, as this is the core of place-based learning.

---

[20] Noel Gough argues that he cannot imagine place '*being*' pedagogical but 'can imagine "places" (as specific locations) *becoming* "pedagogical"' (2009: 155–6, emphasis in original).

[21] For criteria and performance descriptors to assess sense of place, see Demarest (2015: 133–4).

Place is thus a complex, open-ended phenomenon, generated by (and capable of generating) interactions between physical environments, humans, their social contexts and cultural texts, more-than-humans, memories, imagination and cognition. It cannot ever be (or stay) just one thing as it is generated through the interaction of some or all of these parts. It is, in Edward Soja's words, both real and imagined (1996: 11). Its complexity and variability make it an exciting, challenging and dynamic partner for exploring Shakespeare. If we recognise that place is an experience felt differently by each of our learners and capable of change, then it becomes an opportunity for everyone to access Shakespeare on their own terms while enriching their own sense of place.

REFLECTION IN PLACE

How might these dimensions and modes of place intertwine in the Shakespeare classroom? Let's take Shakespeare's Sonnet 18 as a test case. How might students engage with the sonnet if they first reflected via a relational mode on their emplaced experiences of summer? Learners could begin with a self-reflective writing activity that asked them to revisit the interactions that constituted a memory of summer in a specific place. This engages the fictional landscape of the sonnet in a tangible, localised way, invoking relational place and all three dimensions of setting, material and imagined place. This could be completed in conjunction with site visits to a location where learners reflect on seasonality and place as eventmental (a local nursery, community or school garden). What is planted and what flowers in the summer of the learner's place? When must fruits or foods be harvested in order to maximise their value and prevent their loss and decline? These questions adopt an eventmental mode of place. A localised example of how 'every fair from fair sometimes declines, / By chance or nature's changing course untrimm'd' (7–8) might materialise the sonnet's interest in the brevity of the fertile warm season and the cyclical rhythms of ecological systems and human life. This would underscore the extraordinary claim of the persona in promising an 'eternal summer' through growth in his 'eternal lines' (9, 12). Learners could be asked to rewrite the sonnet with images specific to a place they have experienced in summer (through reflective writing or site visits) – practising place as a way of knowing – and to analyse how the substitution exercise affected the sonnet's meaning. Any or all of these place-based elements require close reading and textual analysis. They benefit from historicist and presentist readings of the text. Place-based Shakespeare enriches these critical thinking skills through asking learners to consider more deeply the presence of place in the text, the presence of the text in place and the interaction between learner, place and text in the Shakespeare classroom.

For this 'Reflection in Place', I invite you to consider:

- How do you define place?
- Do you know how your students perceive or define place?
- How might your students' definition differ or align with yours?
- What dimensions or modes of place are visible in your Shakespeare classrooms, and how do you experience their intersection?
- What kind of preliminary work is needed so that Shakespeare students are better equipped to learn with place?

This section identified four key findings in student reflections on their engagement with place and Shakespeare in regional North Queensland. It also offers a complexivist definition of place as a multifaceted phenomenon comprising many dimensions and modes, and always experienced as a sense of place. The student voices represented in this section demonstrate that introducing place into the Shakespeare classroom will present an immediate and productive challenge to the status quo. Place-based Shakespeare requires us to question the invisibility of place in SysEd and spotlights (perhaps with some discomfort) our band of perceived relevance. It asks us as educators to rethink how we teach and learn, and it invites students to actively reflect on how their learning is embedded in their environmental and cultural contexts.

While this survey canvassed preliminary attitudes to place prior to any actual PBL, the responses illuminate the generative potential of place as an agent in the Shakespeare classroom. Despite the diverse views on place and a dominant belief in the disconnection between lived and literary place, the concept of place sparked provocative learning opportunities. In thinking about place, students evaluated their spatially inflected identity, their social interactions, their methods of learning, the perceived influence of cultural capital and regionality, parallels between social behaviours in Shakespeare and contemporary Australia, the role of Shakespeare in the public sphere, the use of space to unpack Shakespeare's themes and an awareness of the socially constructed nature of place. The richness and diversity of responses indicate the potential value of bringing place to the fore in Shakespeare classrooms.

3 Exploring Place: Experimenting with Outdoor Shakespeare

One August morning in 2018, my first-year English class ventured into the late winter sun, still strong and hot in the tropics, to study Act Four, Scene Three of *As You Like It* – the redemption of Oliver. My students quickly identified how Shakespeare's descriptions of the oak, 'mossed with age', bled into the depiction of the 'wretched ragged man, o'ergrown with hair' (4.3.103–5). They noted allusions to Eden, animal imagery, and queried the veracity of Oliver's tale. But there was no sublime place-induced Shakespearean epiphany. Taking Shakespeare outside must move beyond what Garrard dryly refers to as a kind of vague 'romantic educational theory' (2010: 236).

Section 3 of *Shakespeare and Place-Based Learning* investigates the challenges of using outdoor place to teach Shakespeare through analysis of 'Shakespeare on Site', a series of student theatre workshops facilitated with a local theatre company, TheatreiNQ. Led by TheatreiNQ's education director, Arminelle Fleming, these outdoor workshops took place in two series across 2019 and 2022 (Table 2). By focussing directly on the students' voices, the workshops respond to what has been identified as a 'void in the research' on outdoor education (James & Williams, 2017: 59; Marchant et al., 2019: 3). Participants comprised twenty-five Townsville students in Years 10–12 (ages 15–18) from public and private schools. Workshops were voluntary, took place outside of class and were not related to assessment.

Table 2 'Shakespeare on Site' workshops.

Code	Date	Text	Location
MND	May 2019	*A Midsummer Night's Dream*	Anderson Botanical Gardens
MA	August 2019	*Macbeth*	Jezzine Barracks, Kissing Point
O	September 2019	*Othello*	TheatreiNQ *Othello* outdoor set, Queen's Park
MB	February 2022	*Macbeth*	Jezzine Barracks, Kissing Point
T	February 2022	*The Tempest*	Cape Pallarenda

Note: Each student is coded and numbered by the workshop in which they participated.

Throughout, the students' observations and my own critical reflections illuminate the challenges of designing and implementing effective place-based Shakespeare with outdoor place as a learning partner.

*'Helpful, but Not Essential': Underdetermined and Overdetermined Place in Anderson Botanical Gardens (*A Midsummer Night's Dream*) and Queen's Park (*Othello*)

Two workshops in the 'Shakespeare on Site' series exemplified the challenges faced by place-based educators and provided a critical lesson on how to support PBL in Shakespeare classrooms. The first workshop suffered from an underdetermined role of place, leaving students with no model from which to build their engagement with place and Shakespeare. By contrast, the second workshop's chosen location led to an overdetermined sense of place, with pre-existing links between play and place so explicit that students' own sense of place was not readily invoked.

Figure 2 Anderson Botanical Gardens, location of *A Midsummer Night's Dream* workshop. © Chrissy Maguire.

In the first workshop, students focussed on Act Two, Scene One of *A Midsummer Night's Dream* in Anderson Botanical Gardens (Figure 2). Of the respondents surveyed, 53 per cent indicated they had either studied or seen the play before, and 86 per cent had been to the gardens previously. Participants took part in an introductory discussion of the text (on repetition, alliteration and antithesis) before moving into pairs and selecting locations in the park for rehearsing the scene. There were no discussions about place and no explicit directives around engaging with the location. This was a deliberate choice, as I did not want to colour the students' experience of place or pre-empt what I expected them to find or feel. When asked where they would like to perform, the first pair indicated they had no preference and selected the location they had used for rehearsal. All subsequent pairs used that same space for their performances; the 'stage' had been established and was, in the students' minds, no longer moveable. The place was not open for reimagining or experimentation.

In post-workshop surveys, the participants explicitly noted the effect of the space upon their mood. Vocabulary choices included 'calming' (four students), 'relaxing' (seven students), 'happy', 'peaceful' and 'welcomed' (two students). One student, referred to as MND8 (see Table 2), noted that the location made them feel 'less anxious, really engaged, happy, relaxed, content ... It made me feel relaxed and happier. The open space is far less stressful than an enclosed room.' MND10 reported that the location made them 'relaxed, happy' because 'groups of people indoors makes me feel trapped and anxious'. The outdoor park location appeared to assist students not in their direct understanding of Shakespeare but rather in generating a positive mood which framed their learning experience.

Although the scene is set in the forest outside of Athens and is full of references to the 'wood' (2.1.191–2, 223, 237), only two students directly connected their lived experience of place (the gardens) with the literary place (the woods) of *A Midsummer Night's Dream*. MND6 observed: 'The setting of the play was in the woods so it seemed fitting to do the play in a park. It made the play more enjoyable.' MND12 wrote the location 'suited the nature of plays, as in, emotion'. While these students exhibited a 'place sensitive' awareness, most students experienced what Beames would classify as a 'place ambivalent' PBL, where place is nothing more than a 'staging ground' for activities (Section 1). This is equivalent to Relph's category of 'incidental outsider', for whom place is just a 'background' (1976: 52). This is a common attitude because 'what we are doing frequently overshadows where we are doing it' (Relph, 1976: 52). Respondent MND1 wrote that the location was 'helpful but not eccencial [essential]'. Others reflected: 'Personally, location doesn't have much impact on my understanding' (MND9); 'The course itself didn't rely on location but it was a nice setting regardless' (MND5). The workshop proved valuable not because of a place-based romantic epiphany but the reverse: it revealed that students are not taught to nor expect to engage with place as a learning partner. It falls completely beyond their knowledge, skills and band of perceived relevance, and while it positively impacted mood and confidence, students felt it was irrelevant to the workshop content.

Figure 3 'Shakespeare under the Stars' production of *Othello*, directed by Terri Brabon (TheatreiNQ). Queen's Park, Townsville, 2019. © Chrissy Maguire.

By nature of its location, the *Othello* workshop focussed more pragmatically on performing Shakespeare outdoors. None of the participants were familiar with *Othello*, but 83 per cent of students were familiar with the location. The workshop took place at Queen's Park, within the TheatreiNQ set for their 2019 'Shakespeare under the Stars' outdoor production of *Othello* (Figure 3). The park is the traditional home of their annual outdoor Shakespeare performance. Each year, TheatreiNQ constructs an elaborate set, specific to the needs of the production, within the park. During the workshop, participants were taken on a tour of the stage space, seating bank and backstage areas.

Students indicated the importance of this location because of its function as a 'real' set for *Othello*: the set 'really puts you into the story' (O1); the location 'of the actual performance ... helped us feel a part of the story' (O3); 'It was great to work on set as it provided a greater understanding to the play and helped with correct projection' (O2); 'the set made it easier to picture the play' (O6); and 'I think that being in the space made me enjoy it more, as it was more exciting and engaging. The set made me feel connected to the time period and story' (O3).

The professional set appears to have eased the imaginative and cognitive burden for the students, enhancing their ability to engage with the 'story' and making it '*easier* to picture' the play. But because the set itself linked place and play, it is possible that this constrained the development of idiosyncratic connections between the students' experience of the play and sense of place. Student O3 reflected that, of the three workshop sites in 2019, this was their preferred place: 'Queen's gardens was more effective, as we had the opportunity to perform on the real stage'. Because the set was 'real', it was interpreted as a deeper, more authentic means of connecting Shakespeare to place. Overwhelmingly students' attention was centred on the set, not the park. Only two students connected to the park more broadly. O5 wrote: 'I have a close connection with Shakespeare and Queens Gardens', and O4 identified a relationship between the workshop's location and the play in 'the set, of course, and the natural environments'. Choosing a theatre set for this workshop focussed participants on the business of staging rather than their own idiosyncratic sense of place. While several students indicated that the location helped them 'picture' the play and feel 'a part' of the story, they were picturing and feeling 'a part' of a vision for a specific production. Overwhelmingly, place was over-determined and operated as a background or vehicle for the theatrical construction of Shakespeare's story. This flatter, pre-constructed idea of place positioned the location as serving the play, rather than allowing place agential status as a partner in the learning process.

These two early workshops taught me an important lesson as a Shakespeare educator working with place. Despite taking place outdoors, both workshops suffered from a sense of placelessness. Place-based scholars have drawn attention to this 'ethos of placelessness in education' (Ball & Lai, 2006: 264; Bartholomaeus, 2013: 18; Gruenewald, 2003a: 317; Gruenewald and Smith, 2014b: xvi; Wattchow & Brown, 2011: 24).

Somerville and colleagues wonder if 'as a society we erase a sense of place in our schools rather than teaching with it' (2009: 4). Placelessness refers to an 'insensitivity to the significance of place' (Relph, 1976: preface). It overrides the distinctiveness of places with standardised place, diluting the experience of being in a specific place and creating a homogenised sense of place where places 'not only look alike but feel alike' and offer the same possibilities for experience (Relph, 1976: 90). This 'erosion of place' leads to an anonymous universalised space that 'could be anywhere', detached from the local environment (Cresswell, 2015: 75). Student responses at both workshops indicated that these places could indeed have been anywhere. The park was an undifferentiated backdrop, viewed as not 'essential' with little 'impact'. The outdoor set generated a sense of place in service to the play; it was valued for its status as a stage with minimal engagement with the place itself. Despite my intention to incorporate place, placelessness persisted. In light of this, 'how can education become "rooted" in place when place itself is increasingly ephemeral, non-existent, or untethered to a geolocation? This question is a defining ontological and epistemological question for place-based education in supermodernity' (Bertling, 2018: 1628).

This experience of 'non-place' (Nakagawa & Payne, 2017) presents 'fundamental and existential challenges to the field of place-based education' (Bertling, 2018: 1628). To counter these challenges in Shakespeare class-rooms, starting with an acknowledgement of placelessness can be powerful. In one iteration of his undergraduate 'Sense of Place' unit, which he developed over the course of twelve years, John F. Cameron devoted a class to 'issues of placelessness and displacement' and reported a powerful response from students about alienation, grief and loss of place (2014: 292, 293). Some expressed a sense of shame or failure in 'not having a sense of place', and many chose to write passionate essays on the topic (2014: 292). Cameron's reflection acknowledges that the place-based classroom must also give space to acknowledge loss and alienation (2014: 292). Given that place falls far outside students' bands of perceived relevance, space should also be given to explicitly recognise the potential discomfort, resistance and risk involved in engaging with place in the Shakespeare classroom.

Moving Shakespeare classes to place-specific settings will not, on its own, override the placelessness of education. Outdoor education must also be accompanied by a model of place relations that enriches – without overdetermining – a learner's sense of place.

'It Gave the Script Life': Connecting Place and Play at Kissing Point (Macbeth)

In both the 2019 and 2022 series of 'Shakespeare on Site', a *Macbeth* workshop was held at Jezzine Barracks, Kissing Point, a historical World War II military site on the Townsville coastline. This site offered the potential to generate significant connections between *Macbeth* and early modern and twentieth-century militarisation – connections drawn out insightfully by Randall Martin's ecological analysis of the play, which links it to gunpowder warfare and 'mechanised war' (2015: 106; see also Harris, 2007). Across both 'Shakespeare on Site' workshops held at the barracks, 100 per cent of students indicated that they had previously visited the location and 40 per cent were familiar with *Macbeth*.

Unlike the *MND* workshop in the Botanical Gardens, for *Macbeth* in 2019 students were explicitly invited to connect the script with their immediate place. They were tasked with finding an 'interesting location' to perform Act Two, Scene Two of *Macbeth*, which TheatreiNQ's education director Arminelle Fleming indicated takes place in an enclosed space. The four pairs picked diverse locations. Pair one chose the historic battery guns at the Kissing Point Fortification (Figure 4); pair two found a narrow, concrete stairway; pair three chose a space in front of the entry to the World War II gun stores; and pair four chose an open space with views across to the ocean. By inviting students to consider place as a part of the workshop experience, and giving them the choice to find their own locations for the scene, participants reported stronger connections with place.

The facilitator's encouragement to consider the location in terms of the action and language of the scene generated connections between the students' place and *Macbeth*: 'we used the space to unleash the meaning' (MA3); 'the secluded locations suited the scene' (MA6). Participant MA1 wrote: 'It [the location] got me in the mood of *Macbeth* in some areas. It made me feel intrigued. It helped me understand the story more. The small

Figure 4 Cannon at Kissing Point, Townsville. © Chrissy Maguire.

areas made it feel more tense.' This student connected their embodied experience in place with the 'mood' of *Macbeth*; her choice of 'intrigued' and 'tense' reflects the tone of the dialogue between Macbeth and Lady Macbeth in this scene. Student MA5 made a similar connection, writing that: 'There were some enclosed space signifying how Macbeth felt boxed in.' The use of spatial terminology provides an insightful interpretation of Macbeth's psychological state at this moment of the play; he is 'brainsickly' (2.2.47) and 'lost' in his thoughts (2.2.72–3), 'afraid to think what I have done' (2.2.52) and alarmed by 'every noise' (2.2.59). Students linked the location not only to character but also to context and setting. Participant MA4 noted the location 'fit the setting of Macbeth because of military setting', connecting the historical context of their place to the battles in *Macbeth*. Participant O6 wrote: 'My favourite [workshop] was Macbeth at Jezzine Barracks because of the real military locations, that really made the scenes come to life and feel real.' Jezzine Barracks generated insights into character and context, demonstrating that students can make thematic and psychological connections between their place and the mood, characterisation, setting and action of a text.

Appropriate scaffolding is needed to incorporate place in the Shakespeare classroom. The connections between play and place are not straightforward. As Gretchen E. Minton observes in her dramaturgy of a 'global warming *Macbeth*', the links 'between Shakespeare's sense of ecological crisis and our own' are complex (2018: 432). While students engaged with place to interpret and understand *Macbeth*, they did not use the text to enhance their understanding of place or their environmental responsibilities. The *Macbeth* workshop generated deeper engagements with place, but it was far from optimal PBL. Had these workshops been linked to student coursework, students' insights on place could have been concretised and further developed with preliminary work (such as pre-reading on the history of the Barracks or the historical sources of *Macbeth*) and subsequent assessment tasks that enhanced their place-based reflections.

In 2022, we returned to the same site with the same *Macbeth* scene (Figure 5). In this workshop, Fleming and I were explicit about place as a part of the work. Before students selected their location to rehearse and perform the scene (Figure 6), Fleming asked the students to think about 'how we use the place we're in to perform the scene'. Preliminary discussion focussed on the settings of *Macbeth*. Initial student responses to the question of setting included the 'castle', 'Scotland' and 'near the King's chamber'. Place is always more than one thing; all the answers were different, correct, and offered multiple connotations for interpreting this scene and *Macbeth*. Fleming then asked the students to populate the setting. Suggestions from the students included a tapestry; candles; wood; curtains on the bed; empty floorspace; a big bed; empty room; stone; timber; heavy fabrics; dark; and smoky. When asked what a castle was made of, timber and stone were offered. In considering the difference between Scotland and Australia, responses included 'it's cold'; 'fireplace'; and 'Vikings!'. Students offered examples of *Brave* and *Harry Potter* (which feature castles in Scotland and England) to explain their imagined response to the setting of *Macbeth*. This speaks to learners' 'multi-layered identities' and how sense of place is 'interwoven' alongside multiple experiences of places and cultures (Green & Clark, 2013: 4). It reinforces that pop culture may be more familiar than local

Figure 5 Students rehearse *Macbeth* under the trees at Kissing Point, Townsville. © Chrissy Maguire.

Figure 6 A student rehearses *Macbeth* at Kissing Point, Townsville. © Chrissy Maguire.

places and texts (such as Australian literary texts or works local to the North Queensland region) and that cultural texts like those mentioned by the students may be understood as 'places' for young people: sites where cultural values are communicated and explored (Stevenson, 2008: 354). This engagement with imagined place also demonstrates 'vicarious insideness', a deeply felt, second-hand experience of place, often conveyed by artists and experienced through media such as film (Relph, 1976: 52–3). This preliminary discussion activated the dimensions of setting and imagined place.

On reflecting upon their use of place in exploring *Macbeth*, many of the students connected the location to the earlier discussion of the castle. In particular, the 'stone' construction of the castle played out across students' minds as they imagined the space and performed the scenes. Participant MB4 described the location: 'Lots of old stone structures, like the castle in Macbeth', while MB3 discussed the 'historical' importance of the 'cement objects'. Participant MB8 wrote: 'The scene is set in a stone castle, similar to the stone wall at Jezzine Barracks', adding: 'My partner and I chose the semi-circle shaped, stone wall surrounding a canon. We chose this place as it had the similar stone walls my partner and I were envisioning in the scene. It had fantastic echo for us to play with and an interesting shape we could work some movement around.'

The material place of Jezzine Barracks was pertinent because it matched the students' imagined sense of place – what they 'were envisioning' for *Macbeth*. They also thought about the practicalities of material place for performance through its acoustics and shape (Figure 7). Participant MB9 was also attentive to the materiality of the place: 'I chose to work in a very small concrete slab . . . because we thought it would be fun to work in such a small and intimate place' (Figure 8). The links between play and place were dominated by the opening discussion; the framing of the class strongly influenced the way participants interacted with and reflected on place.

This focus on the material dimension of place reinforces several learnings for a place-based educator. First, students are untrained in using place as an agent in the learning experience, and their interactions can be influenced by the educator's sense of place. This requires careful

Figure 7 Student explores a staircase at Kissing Point, Townsville. © Chrissy Maguire.

Figure 8 Students rehearse in the cannon area at Kissing Point, Townsville. © Chrissy Maguire.

framing that models but does not overdetermine or predetermine a learner's engagement with place. An unexpected conversation about construction of medieval castles resonated at the forefront of many students' thinking in this workshop. However, without any pre-class discussion or framing, students may feel less confident in bridging what may be perceived as a distance between play and place. Place-based teaching and learning are thus skills that require practice. And like any learning experience, it is never entirely predictable.

There was no facilitator-led discussion of the historical background or meaning of the site we had chosen. Yet 30 per cent of students made connections between *Macbeth* and the military location. Student MB3 twice described the location as 'historical' as a way of explaining the links between place and play, while MB5 articulated the relationship between *Macbeth* and Kissing Point: 'Macbeth is set in a castle in Scotland, and Kissing Point was good for recreating this scenery with the old army base.' This demonstrates the students' ability to begin to identify the stories of place (Section 1). The World War II fort speaks specifically to North Queensland's twentieth-century history and its legacies of conflict. If this workshop had allowed for future assessment, further work could have been conducted on investigations of the fort and parallels between military histories of play and place.

The location of the workshop also influenced the students' imaginative capacity and engagement with the text. Students MB2 and MB7 reflected on Kissing Point's impact on the script: 'it made the scene more alive'; 'it gave the script life'. Several students found the place supportive of what they self-identified as creativity and imagination: MB3 said the place made her feel 'Creative, it made me think about how I could use different things . . . [the location] made me think about the space and how it could be used and imagined'. Participant MB4 felt the location 'helped me to feel like I was in a fictional world due to the lack of recognisable buildings'. Participant MB5 felt the location 'was good for giving me lots of ideas when doing Macbeth scenes'. In particular, they felt it was 'easier than working in a flat, enclosed space' because it was 'helpful to understand scenery in the outdoors'. For MB7, the location 'helped me picture the castle'. The 'outdoors, stone and echo' of the location made MB8 feel 'inspired, creative, into the scene', which 'felt realistic'. This student reflected that they 'play[ed] with the surroundings (this changes how I performed the scene)'. Of course, not all students felt this way: MB10 preferred 'private settings' to avoid seeing people they knew and for 'airconditioning' (a reasonable request in a Queensland summer), and MB1 reflected that although 'the quietness put my mindset more into the workshop ... however the shade or the apmasfere [atmosphere] didn't sit right IDK [I don't know] why'. The workshop's location overwhelmingly produced a more immersive experience for students, who felt transported into the play's 'fictional world' as they imagined it, were 'into the scene' and felt that the scene was 'realistic' and 'alive' because of their experience of place. Place aided in the production of ideas around the play and performance. While this is a testament to its potential for teaching Shakespeare, it is important to remember that place is more than a vehicle for communicating learning; it is also an agent, and its stories must be listened to and respected. It should be both topic and teacher. The *Macbeth* workshop, while activating place as an agent in the learning process, failed to utilise the text to deepen understanding of place and the participants' responsibilities to it. As such, it is *partial* PBL; but as noted in the introduction to this Element, imperfect PBL is inevitable. Place-based educators should consider their practice as an ongoing learning process that continually builds a deeper knowledge of and respect for place.

'It Moves Underneath You': Contested Place and Embodiment at Cape Pallarenda (The Tempest)

The final workshop of the 'Shakespeare on Site' series took place at Freemasons Park, Cape Pallarenda (Figure 9). Described as a 'hidden gem' by one of the participants, it is quieter than the more central beaches. The students had diverse histories with Cape Pallarenda, reinforcing the idiosyncrasy of a learner's sense of place. Student T1 reflected that 'Pallarenda doesn't have any major significance for me. In my opinion, it belongs to the children that frequent the parks, and the locals that live on the beachfront.' But to T3: 'The wildlife and beach mean a lot to me and

Figure 9 The students arrive at Cape Pallarenda. © Chrissy Maguire.

my family as we have grown up here.' They described how their family volunteered in wildlife rescue and used this area to source much-needed flora for recovering native animals. Their sense of place was explicitly tied to a sense of environmental responsibility. The contrast between T1 and T3 exemplifies Relph's insider–outsider dualism, one that he believes 'is fundamental to our experience of lived-space and one that provides the essence of place' (1976: 49). This connection or lack thereof, though, did not prevent the students from forming connections between place and play. Participant T1, who felt the site was insignificant personally, nevertheless reflected that 'It made me feel more connected to the characters and their situations', while for T3, 'It felt genuine and almost easier to act because it was happening as we spoke rather than having [to] transport yourself into a headspace like the beach'. This suggests that diverse experiences and knowledges of place do not necessarily predetermine how a learner may benefit from the place of learning.

Figure 10 Rehearsal of the 'log scene' (3.1) in *The Tempest*. © Chrissy Maguire.

None of the students had studied *The Tempest* before. In this workshop, they looked at Act Three, Scene One, where Miranda expresses her love for Ferdinand as he carries logs for Prospero (Figure 10). The scene was chosen by TheatreiNQ as it was ideal for pairs and allowed the opportunity to play with props. Preliminary discussion and readings of the scene, led by Fleming and me, canvassed both text and context. We considered the arrival of the characters to the island, compared this to the concept of 'boat people' (a politically loaded term in Australia) and the arrival of settler colonists to Australia in the eighteenth century, and thought about this in relation to Caliban, postcolonialism and shipwrecks. This conversation was unrehearsed and improvisational, with facilitators and students seated around a picnic table. The students did not seek to expand the discussion of European invasion and white settlement in their consideration of *The Tempest*'s depiction of an invaded island. They were preoccupied by the prospect of shipwreck and the dangers of ocean travel. Reflecting on their experience of boat travel, one student commented: 'on a boat at night it's so scary, you can only see blackness'. While my sense of place at Cape Pallarenda was predominantly focussed on its colonial past and the violent but still too-often invisible histories of this legacy, the students did not proactively engage with this spatial link between *The Tempest* and Townsville. This indicates the complexity and multiplicity of place, and the problem of potential disconnection from a place and its histories.

This discussion of Australian colonial history and *The Tempest* exemplifies a crux at the heart of PBL. We know that the meaning of place is unstable. In the words of one student in relation to the Cape Pallarenda sand, 'it moves underneath you'. The Townsville I know is vastly different from the Townsville familiar to the workshop participants. 'Places are never just one place'; they are 'fluid and contested terrain' (Greenwood, 2019: 364; 2013: 94). Teaching and learning about place inevitably mean 'participating in a contact zone of difference', an intersection of 'culturally different and often contested stories of place' (Somerville et al., 2011: 6). This makes it impossible to standardise place-based Shakespeare because it must be specific to the learners' sense of place (Gruenewald, 2003b: 644). We cannot 'stay in our place – we need to go to theirs' (Demarest, 2015: 7). But what if, in going to theirs, we overlook dimensions of place that have been rendered invisible or marginalised? The 'Shakespeare on Site' workshops were designed to be learner-led, to 'go to their place' and explore how learners engaged with place with minimal framing to colour their interactions. My aim was to prevent privileging 'certain interpretations' of place, where an educator projects their desires for 'what they want a place to be', and thus unintentionally circumscribes its potential (Wattchow & Brown, 2011: 25). *The Tempest* workshop attempted a balance between underdetermined and overdetermined place, but it raised an important, vexed question for place-based educators: how do we find the right balance between engaging and respecting a student's existing sense of place (as complex as that is) and challenging their sense of place in order to illuminate dimensions of place that may enhance and deepen their engagement and civic responsibility? While participants at *The Tempest* workshop engaged in a discussion that touched on postcolonialism in

The Tempest and in reference to Australia's white settler histories, they were not given enough framing or time to develop a deep understanding of this relationship or to seriously develop their sense of place.

For a focussed, extended place-based course where an educator wants their students to consider *The Tempest* in relation to Australia's colonial history, participants could have been given pre-workshop reading or questions to frame their experience at Cape Pallarenda. I model here Demarest's approach to PBL which asks educators to consider: 'what do you want your students to know before you go?' (pre-visit), 'What do you want your students to learn while they are there?' (on-site) and 'What do you want your students to consider/learn after the visit?' (post-visit) (Demarest, 2015: 116). For this workshop, students could have been given historical information about the European settlement of Queensland, particularly its history of 'blackbirding' (Stead & Altman, 2019) and the significance of Cape Pallarenda to Indigenous peoples and within white settler histories. This could have been accompanied by postcolonial and blue humanities pre-readings on *The Tempest* as well as Sea Country (Mentz, 2009, 2015; Whitehouse et al., 2014). On-site, students could have been asked to reflect on their knowledge of Queensland's colonial history and the role ocean travel played in this, as well as the relationship between colonisation and Indigenous labour. This may have reframed the interpretation of a prince carrying logs across hot sand. Post-visit, learners could have written reflective statements considering how place informed their understanding of *The Tempest* and how enacting scenes from the play fed back into their knowledge of the historical and cultural dimensions of place.

In the physical difficulties that attended this workshop unexpectedly lay the bones of a successful engagement with place as a learning partner. The Cape Pallarenda workshop was the most physically challenging of the 'Shakespeare on Site' series. The beach was hot, open, exposed, glary, noisy and windy. A harsh summer sun scoured the beach and a gusty breeze threatened to whip away our scripts. Physicality and embodiment quickly became central to the workshop. Fleming provided log props, telling the students: 'use whatever is going on in the scene. If your hat flies away – use it. If the sea gets noisy, use it!' Shoes were quickly

Figure 11 Ferdinand and Miranda contend with the elements at Cape Pallarenda. © Chrissy Maguire.

abandoned. The sand, though, was hot and unsteady on bare feet. I asked the students how it felt to stage the scene here: 'awkward', 'hot' and 'hard to put the movement in'. At one point, a bee interrupted the performance. A student playing Ferdinand stepped on dried coral. Quickly, the log-carrying duties of Ferdinand became difficult and even unpleasant. The challenges of Ferdinand's 'log-man' duties (3.1.67) were discussed extensively (Figure 11). 'The wood creates a good prop when Miranda says something out of nowhere', commented one student. 'So when she says she wants to marry me – just stopping, or your grip loosening a bit, that would be great.' The sand also became a point of discussion. 'You have to catch yourself a lot on sand', reflected one student. 'It moves underneath you. Usually it's done in an auditorium on hard surfaces.' 'But that adds to it', responded a student, noting that it enhanced the 'clumsiness' of the characters. One student observed that the ocean and 'wind made us louder'. In a post-workshop survey, T2 commented: 'It was hot windy and loud but I feel it added to the scene and believability. . . . it was hard physically but easier drama wise.' This workshop made clear that 'the places of performance', and, I would add, places of learning, 'with their weather conditions, flora and fauna – are crucial to reception' (Martin & O'Malley, 2015: 382). The unexpected, unpleasant elements of the site altered participants' interpretation of the scene and its characters. This minor (albeit at times painful) positive turbulence generated productive learning.

Almost none of the students enjoyed the environment, but they none-theless identified the value of this physical challenge for engaging in the dramatic interpretation of the scene: 'it [performing the scene] became more enjoyable', said T1. Student T2 wrote: 'it is a learning experience but it was kinda hard, as it was hot and hard to focus', but she added that the location 'help[ed] cause it shows what it would be like'. Potentially the elements of this place – the logs, loose sand, sharp coral, strong wind, loud surf, insect life and heat – operated as interactive agents, giving the students more to respond to and engage with, which is why despite it being 'hard physically', this place-based Shakespeare workshop was also 'easier drama wise'. This correlates with Wattchow and Brown's prior-itisation of a 'felt, embodied encounter with a place' (2011: 217). Place here was unpredictable, with multiple agents engaged as part of the learning experience.

Students are not trained to engage with place. When completing their post-workshop surveys in 2022, several students asked me for clarification about the questions asked. One said: 'I don't know how I feel about this place.' Another asked: 'What does this question mean?' Learners may struggle to articulate their relationship to place because of a long-standing oversight in how we incorporate place into our pedagogies. In the second *Macbeth* workshop, MB1 was unable to express why she felt the atmosphere did not match the scene: 'IDK why.' At Cape Pallarenda, T1 found learning 'more enjoyable' in the outdoor location but was 'not sure how to explain it'. This may align with Wattchow and Brown's observation that cognition is prioritised in experiential learning over 'more embodied ways of knowing as participants struggle to articulate how they felt about the experience' (2011: 102). The act of consciously considering place as an agent in the learning process is a challenge in itself; it is powerfully invisible even though it is a shaping force in our lives.

REFLECTION IN PLACE

For this 'Reflection in Place', I invite you to consider:

- What are the opportunities and limitations of the place/s in which you currently teach?
- What outdoor places have you, or might you, engage as a partner in a place-based Shakespeare classroom?
- How might you respect a balance between a learner's existing sense of place and the learning opportunities that will deepen and enrich that sense of place?
- How might you plan a place-based Shakespeare lesson using Demarest's pre-visit, on-site and post-visit stimulus questions?

After each 'Shakespeare on Site' workshop, students were asked the same question: 'Was today's location important in helping you to understand or enjoy the workshop?' (Figure 12). Across all workshops, participants indicated an overwhelmingly positive response to the role of place in their learning.

As educators, we must tread a fine line in introducing PBL to our Shakespeare classrooms; our own sense of place cannot overdetermine and pre-empt the connections students may make. But conversely, groundwork is needed to facilitate students' ability to make their own connections and to enrich a student's sense of place. Our approach to place must thus be 'deliberate' (Bass et al., 2020: 21) but not overdetermined. Lesson planning must be carefully constructed; as I explored in *The Tempest* workshop, the way an educator chooses to frame a place-based lesson (historical context of play or place, contemporary sociopolitics, physical environment and so on) can powerfully guide a student's place-based experiences. Place-based educators need to balance multiple facets of place within a Shakespeare class, including a student's preconceived sense of place, setting, the

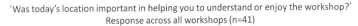

'Was today's location important in helping you to understand or enjoy the workshop?'
Response across all workshops (n=41)

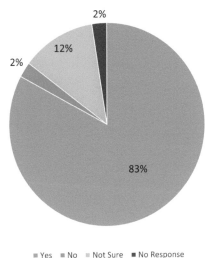

■ Yes ■ No ■ Not Sure ■ No Response

Figure 12 'Shakespeare on Site' post-workshop survey (2019–22).

requirements of a scene, the learning outcomes and the lived place in which learning occurs.

We must also trust in the ability of learners to generate their own connections. This, of course, can only happen if place is perceived as part of the learning process and not outside the band of perceived relevance (Section 2). Learners bring their own diverse experiences of place, whether this is intertextual knowledge or histories and memories. In 'Shakespeare on Site', participants identified a range of connections between play and place: historical links; the tangible material of the space; its intangible ability to generate creativity and immersion; and its thematic potential. Learners are also, when given the opportunity, able to make critical reflections on their experience of place. In response to the question, 'Is your location important when it comes to learning about Shakespeare?', O6 responded:

> In a classroom with just a teacher saying things at a room of uninterested people, and the endgoal being assessment, it is hard to enjoy learning Shakespeare. A setting like this [the *Othello* stage in Queen's Park] which is interactive and inclusive of everyone really helps me become more interested in what is being taught. ... being outdoors can help release pressure in learning environments. (O6)

Participant O6 unintentionally identified a host of core tenets of PBL: genuine lifelong learning; teaching beyond the test; community, interactivity and inclusivity; and learner engagement.

4 Learning Place: A Model for Teaching Place-Based Shakespeare

Central to my approach to PBL is the learner's sense of place. This does not always mean beginning PBL 'with places that students already have strong affective connections to' (Loh, 2018: n.p.); it means beginning by respecting a learner's sense of place and providing the means for its enrichment. This is essential for genuine engagement with place. As Shakespearean PBL invites learners to engage with their own sense of place, it works to share power 'by acknowledging the experience and other forms of knowledge and expertise that students bring to the classroom' (Dadabhoy & Mehdizadeh, 2023: 16). This is a 'student-centred' approach, which is 'not about abandoning students to whatever interests them, leaving Shakespeare's text at the periphery' (Thompson & Turchi, 2016: 10). It is about inviting learners to connect to Shakespeare's texts through their sense of place, which is itself developed through this process, enriching a part of human identity that shapes how we move through the world. Sense of place is co-constituted with the texts learners encounter: students use Shakespeare's texts to interpret their place, while their experience of place informs their study of Shakespeare (Charlton et al., 2011: 67; Green, 2013: 28). This mutually enriching bidirectional mode of PBL engages literature to understand place and sense of place to understand literature (Fischer, 2015: 13; Loh, 2018).

While an exploration of a student's 'personal sense of place is an effective first step of using place in the English classroom', it must be accompanied by a 'critical frame' (Azano, 2011: 10). My model (Figure 13) is informed by the critical frameworks articulated in Section 1. It is founded on a complexivist sense of place that is generated and sustained by interactions. In guiding learners to consider multiple places, it is informed by Greenwood's goals of decolonisation and reinhabitation and Somerville's contact zone. It aligns

Figure 13 A model for implementing place-based learning in Shakespeare education.

with Greenwood's six practices for place-consciousness, adapted from Wattchow and Brown's signposts: being present in/with/to place, experiencing place stories, exploring place politics, learning from place, caring for place and representing place (Greenwood, 2019: 365). With an overarching aim of environmental awareness, the model also aligns with ecocritical imperatives of environmental responsibility.

There are four objectives underpinning this model:

1. Deepen a learner's knowledge of and engagement with Shakespeare's texts.
2. Build a learner's core skills in close reading, interdisciplinarity, self-reflexivity and critical thinking.
3. Expand a learner's environmental awareness and sense of environmental and social responsibility.
4. Enrich a learner's personal, authentic engagement with place (sense of place).

Figure 13 visualises the process of place-based learning in Shakespeare studies. It begins from the learner's 'Sense of Place' in relation to the 'Text'. This interaction is positioned as the core of any place-based Shakespeare. This model builds outwards, incorporating learning around 'Dimensions' of place (Material, Setting, Imagined) and 'Modes' of place (ways of Knowing, Eventmental and Relational). As I outlined in Section 1, these Dimensions and Modes are not exhaustive, and their interaction will produce further iterations of both. The model supports multiplicity of place, encouraging learners to engage with a place through different 'dimensions' or 'frames', from political to economic, historical to aesthetic (Greenwood, 2019: 364; Wattchow & Brown, 2011: 125). Exploration of these frames is supported through diverse educational 'Practices', which comprise activities to achieve the outer circle's twin 'Learning Goals' of deepening a learner's knowledge of and engagement with Shakespeare's texts while expanding their environmental awareness and sense of responsibility. The diagram is multidirectional because place-based work should not only start from a learner's sense of place but enrich and develop it. The Learning Goals should feed back into and enrich the learner's Sense of Place. While this model is anthropocentric in centring on a learner's dynamic sense of place, it is in the learner's engagement with PBL that anthropocentrism should be challenged as the learner listens to other voices through recognition of more-than-human elements of place, building a multiperspectival understanding of place.

In this final Section, I illustrate five Practices for incorporating place into Shakespeare classrooms. The first four Practices each pair with a single dimension or mode of place: site reading and setting, outdoor education and imagined place, creative activities and material place, community engagement and relational place. The final Practice – virtual activities – illustrates how PBL inevitably engages multiple dimensions and modes of place. Far from exhaustive and designed to work in complementary ways, these activities indicate the potential for PBL in Shakespeare and English education.

Site Reading and Setting

I adopt Wyse's term of 'site reading' to account for forms of PBL that focus on the fictional settings and places of literary texts (2021: 4). This approach aims to deepen understanding of 'the complex workings of place in narrative texts' in terms of literary knowledge and geospatial and environmental awareness (2021: 6). Site reading is predicated on the understanding that places 'almost always have a concrete form'. 'Even imaginary places, like Hogwarts School in the *Harry Potter* novels, have an imaginary materiality of rooms, staircases, and tunnels that make the novel work' (Cresswell, 2015: 14). This focus on representations of place in literary texts might lead to activities where learners identify the characteristics of settings in relation to the mobility of characters, with 'empathic activities' to develop perspectives on others' situationality (Koessler & Perduca, 2019: 119). When thinking about Shakespearean site reading, we can examine multiple facets of the plays' fictional settings, from the national to domestic, from public, private, internal or external place to the gesture of place names (Berry, 2016: xv) and figurative and symbolic representations of place.

In 2022, I convened a course for senior undergraduates on environments in early modern English literature. In their module on *The Tempest* and the blue humanities (see Mentz, 2019), students participated in a site reading tutorial comprising two parts. The first examined Caliban's experience of the island. Students looked at an excerpt (1.2.320–375) and were asked:

- What do we learn about the history of Caliban?
- How would you stage Caliban's first scene?
- How do the characters relate to the island?
- How do they think about the place in which they live?
- What role does education and language play on the island?
- How does Caliban speak, and how would you describe his language?

After a discussion of the representation of Caliban and his relation to the island, students moved to an outdoor space on campus, with the following prompt:

> How do you feel about the island's ownership (Caliban: 'this island's mine'), given we are learning about this text on a different island, on unceded Aboriginal land marred by centuries of conflict and dispossession of country? Spend 5 minutes doing some reflective writing on your response to this. As you write, reflect on what you see around you, and how you feel about this in terms of some of the issues raised in *The Tempest*: belonging, exposure, the land as nourishing or punishing, etc.

For one tutorial, we took students to sit on the grass beside the campus creek; the aim was to think about land *and* water. Students wrote steadily, and afterwards reported this as one of their preferred tutorials. I pre-empted the activity by informing students that they were not required to submit their work; this was an opportunity for ungraded, private reflection to develop their sense of place in relation to material place and text, site reading and setting.

There are many forms of site reading in a Shakespeare classroom. Amy Azano outlines a PBL scaffolding activity where students engage with texts that might evoke their own sense of place, using creative texts (like country songs) as models for their own place pieces (2011: 6–7). Fischer provides a host of literary place-based pedagogical approaches, including the display of objects that represent 'the narrative fabric of the place and the fluidity of children's real and fictional environments' to spark place-conscious discussion (2015: 20). Thompson and Turchi also provide activities around setting: students can 'imagine and create a new setting' for *The Merchant of Venice* and discuss 'which setting' of *A Midsummer Night's Dream* 'seems more like the one they live in' (2016: 118, 141). In using a place-based approach to teach *A Midsummer Night's Dream*, I focussed on the transition from Athens to the woods, and asked students to reimagine a place that the lovers might escape to via creative writing tasks. This activity tended to collide students' lived experience of place with Shakespeare's use of setting; students responded with locations including airports, meaningful places remembered from childhood holidays, imagined places and natural sites that (as one student wrote) 'have always been important elements for me in life' (2019, in-class work). In another activity with secondary students studying in Charters Towers (remote North Queensland) on the same play, I asked Year 12 students where they would go if they fled Athens. One student responded, wistfully, that she would go to the Torres Strait. Her home. It was then that I learned of remote Queensland boarding schools hosting students from the Torres Strait. This small moment was a profound learning experience for me, as I reflected on Australian educational policy, of learning far from home, of Indigenous students travelling significant distances to access secondary schooling. This was one fleeting example of how PBL in literary studies teaches more than the text.

Outdoor Education and Imagined Place

Perhaps the most literal incarnation of PBL is outdoor education, or a focus on the use of physical space to generate learning about literary texts.[22] Over the past two decades, outdoor education has demonstrated 'positive effects' on personal and social development, academic achievement, leadership and physical activity (Becker et al., 2017: 1; Marchant et al., 2019). While there is

---

[22] In addition to outdoor education, other physical environments should also be considered: an example of the use of indoor space in Shakespeare pedagogy is 'open space' learning (Monk et al., 2011).

no 'all-encompassing' definition of outdoor education, which varies in understanding and practice across countries and cultures (Becker et al., 2017: 2), it is more complex than simply being outside and active. Outdoor education is 'about helping people learn about themselves, how they relate to other people and the environment' (Wattchow & Brown, 2011: 13).[23] Modes include one-off field trips, repeated visits in a chosen place to build an ongoing relationship (Cameron, 2014: 285; Gough, 2009: 169; Wattchow & Brown, 2011: 134), 'bush regeneration, exploratory walks, learning place history and ecology', meditation and quiet observation (Cameron, 2014: 293).

One version of outdoor education in literary studies is the site visit, which connects the place of a literary text with its real-life counterpart by 'visiting some of their important settings' (Moyle, 2017: 112). This is limited to students in easy reach of such locations (Green, 2013: 30–1). Site visits begin not from the lived places of the learner but rather from lived places fictionalised in the text. While this can be enlightening and productive, it is at risk of reductively approaching place entirely in a literal sense, and thus effacing the multiplicity of place. It is also limited in applicability to texts which choose real-life, accessible locations for their settings, and thus may not always be feasible for Shakespeare studies.

The simplest way of trialling outdoor education is to move classes outside to an accessible and usable space, with clear learning objectives and outcomes in mind (see Section 3, especially Demarest's three-part plan). In 2019, I trialled this approach with thirty students enrolled in a Level 2 Shakespeare unit at JCU. My goal was to use outdoor space to support a focus on staging and movement. All Townsville students participated in weekly outdoor tutorials within the outdoor Indigenous Learning Space (Blatman-Thomas, 2019: 1405–6), with students also making use of the surrounding area, which featured picnic tables, a creek, large eucalyptus trees and the frequent presence of brush-turkeys and kangaroos.[24] As part of their

---

[23] For more, see Wattchow and Brown's four signposts for outdoor education (2011: 209).

[24] The Indigenous Learning Space was built in 2013 'to cement the identity of the land' (Blatman-Thomas, 2019: 1411).

assessment, students were organised into 'playing companies' and prepared a short performance and discussion on scenes from *The Taming of the Shrew*, *Much Ado About Nothing*, *Othello* and *Coriolanus* in this outdoor space. In end-of-semester unit reports, several students indicated that 'The structure of the tutorials was especially helpful for understanding each Shakespeare play, and I found that the tutorials were the most beneficial and important part of the subject [unit]. They were not only beneficial for my learning, but also very engaging and enjoyable' (2019, unit report). Eleven students completed an additional survey focussed on their experience of outdoor education. This enabled students to reflect on their learnings and retain the connection to their place-based learning experience (Demarest, 2015: 120). In this survey, 100 per cent of students agreed that the location of the tutorials made a positive difference to their learning. Two main themes became apparent: first, students connected the outdoor space to early modern theatres; and second, the space generated a more informal, relaxed mood. One student emphasised these themes in their comment that: 'The relaxed atmosphere complemented the subject [unit] because Shakespearean plays were often performed in outdoor theatres. This made me want to engage and I felt more connected to the work and the period' ('Remaking Shakespeare' Survey, 2019).

This connection to the early modern period and its staging practices was reinforced by other students: 'It felt like we were closer to the original theatres, performing in daylight and reading over the wind, and the [brush]turkeys.' Another said that the outdoor location 'made us able to understand how playing companies had to adapt to their environments'. This extended to specific aspects of the text: 'I feel like we got a better understanding of the play as a whole, scene directions, and characters. . . . we had to give more thought to staging and imbedded ques. We would not have had this opportunity in a normal classroom' ('Remaking Shakespeare' Survey, 2019). This correlates with results from other outdoor education projects which indicate preferences for learning in outdoor settings, stronger levels of commitment and percep-tions of learning as fun (Becker et al., 2017: 10–11).

In addition to drawing connections between outdoor place and the places of early modern English playing companies, students also detected a change in their confidence and learning behaviours.

I am in my third year with English Lit. as a major and I have never experienced outside learning. I feel that it got the creative juices flowing and encouraged student participation. It also is a less formal approach, and this relaxed me and helped me to look forward to it. I also feel that I was better able to retain content. ('Remaking Shakespeare' Survey, 2019)

Two other students noted that the environment was 'less formal' and 'reduces formality'. For these students, this 'seemed to make everyone comfortable sharing their knowledge and opinions' and made students 'less self-conscious'. This aligns with results from other outdoor education programmes which have detected positive outcomes including 'high self-esteem' and 'growth in self-confidence' (Becker et al., 2017: 11).

Survey results from this small sample overwhelmingly indicated that the outdoor learning space generated two key benefits: a stronger connection to the historical context of Shakespeare's theatre and an increased confidence to stage the plays studied throughout the semester.

Creative Activities and Material Place

Creative activities are common in place-based work. This includes creative writing, nature writing, journals, map drawing, visual arts, 'drawing and painting in place' (Cameron, 2014: 289), youth arts (Somerville et al., 2009: 14) or cultural performance (Mayne, 2009: 186). Creative arts activities can be used to counter stereotypes of a student's place (Gannon, 2009b: 614–15). Place-based writing practices are understood to improve writing skills and empower students, supporting identity development and understanding (Donovan, 2016: 31).[25]

In a unit on environmental literature and ecocriticism, titled 'Green Worlds', I introduced a journaling activity as a component of each student's participation.[26] The journal was a weekly writing task based

---

[25] For place-based writing activities, see Gannon (2009a: 33–6).

[26] For a similar journaling project in a 'Shakespeare and Ecofeminist Theory' course, see Laroche and Munroe (2019: 130).

on a learner's engagement with the required readings and a specific accessible place of their choosing. Regular, repeated visits to place are an important element of genuine PBL (Cameron, 2014: 285; Wattchow & Brown, 2011: 93). Similarly important is student choice in selecting places (Kim & Lee, 2019). In 'Green Worlds', the journals had to demonstrate students' ability to integrate discussion of local place and studied texts.

Students' choice of place was incredibly diverse (partially because the course ran online due to COVID-19). In a class of around twenty-five students, location choices for the journal included a backyard, a grand-parents' farm north of Babinda, a chicken house built by one student's father, Point Peron (Western Australia), a courtyard, a Melbourne apart-ment during lockdown, a back verandah, the path around the Ross River (Townsville), Shields Street in Cairns Central Business District, the ocean, the green spaces of a new suburban development, Magnetic Island, the pontoon on Ross River, the Midnight Hotel in Canberra, a local park, Mauritius and Mount Louisa (Townsville).

I provided weekly writing prompts to facilitate the students' journaling, which included nature writing prompts, exploring the history of their local chosen place, considering how *The Tempest* connected with their environ-ment, creative writing that responded to place and a set text, reflection on a news media publication related to their local environment, discussion of local Indigenous stories, reflection on more-than-human inhabitants and discussions of specific readings and topics like postcolonialism and climate fiction. This models the use of different frames in repeated engagements with place. Some tasks were especially illuminating: as Cameron also reports, students discovered 'how few of the Aboriginal stories remain in most places' (Cameron, 2014: 288).

Despite the low weighting of the assessment, most students engaged deeply, producing carefully curated journals, often beautifully formatted or full of drawings and photographs of their chosen place. While some struggled to build connections between their study of Shakespeare and their place, the personal nature of the task generated authentic reflection on their place and stimulated deeper engagement with the course texts. One student wrote:

In my own environment, I think that reading/watching *The Tempest* and engaging with Gray's work (Gray, 2020) has allowed me to consider the relationships between culture and nature. For example, as I was looking into the history of the River Parks estate park, I found that the land was likely bush land – covered in shrubs, grasses and trees etc. Following the development of the area, it has remained a natural space filled with trees, grasses and other plants. However, in the interest of aesthetics, profits and other human ideas, it was completely reinvented. Most of the trees and plants within the space that grew naturally (without human intervention) were removed. In their place, landscaped gardens, manicured lawns, and other 'natural' elements have been planted. It is interesting to me that a cultural perception of natural beauty would have us tear down nature and 're-do' it. *The Tempest* has increased my awareness of the Anthropocene and allowed me to consider how human ideas have shaped this natural space. ('Green Worlds' journal)

A second assessment task in the same course asked students to 'creatively respond to a local place and a text' encountered in the unit, using notes and reflections from the journal to develop their work. Students were asked to consider how they might 'write back' to what they have read and 'rewrite' place. Several students turned to creative arts. One student created a short film called *Stuck* (Figure 14), taking inspiration from blue humanities scholarship and its framing for *The Tempest* and focussing on the theme of environmental transformation.

The short film tracks the journey of sugarcane, an introduced agricultural species farmed in North Queensland, as it enters a waterway.

Ultimately, *Stuck* offers people the opportunity to reflect on the connection between green fields and blue waterways and the transformations of these landscapes over time. It demands that we think about the actions of the past and present and consider how these might affect the future – especially in terms of how we use and interact with our environment. By

Figure 14 Screenshot of *Stuck* short film (2020). Created for 'Green Worlds' unit at JCU.

> becoming 'stuck' in our local places, we might be able to see the environment just that little bit more clearly. (*Stuck* critical reflection)

This student, embedded in the locality of agricultural Queensland on a family farm, created a poignant and artistically exceptional work that performed place-essential learning, as the text was used to deepen his understanding of place, and place was used to deepen his knowledge of the text.

Another student in this unit created a painting entitled *My Isle* (Figure 15), inspired by reflection on *The Tempest* and her backyard. In her accompanying critical reflection to this artwork (Figure 15), the student used scholarly work to deepen her understanding of place and text.

> David Gray discusses the difference between the island and Milan stating that the play's setting creates a contrast between 'the country (simple, pure) and the city (byzantine, corrupt)' (2). This contrast is what I chose to focus on for my artwork, where my yard is simple and pure and my

Figure 15 'Green Worlds' creative work, entitled *My Isle* (2020).

house (and other aspects of my life) are corrupt. Paul Yachnin states that 'the island is the source of Prospero's power, just as the theater is the source of Shakespeare's; they are places that stand apart from the normal world, places that offer ideal conditions for the conjuring of morally intelligible actions' (Yachnin, 2019). This idea resonated with me as my yard in a sense gives me the power to reflect on and then improve areas of my life. (*My Isle* Critical Reflection)

Although the student reflects that 'none of the play is set in Milan', for her this unseen presence was nonetheless a potent one for *The Tempest*. She compared different responses to the isle and reflected on the subjectivity of our engagement with place:

Shortly after Adrian's description of the air, Gonzalo declares 'how lush and lusty the grass looks. How green!' (Shakespeare, 2011: 2.1.55). However, Antonio argues that by stating 'the ground is indeed tawny' (Shakespeare, 2011: 2.1.56). This difference between how the island is viewed by the characters made me reflect on how I view my yard compared to how other people may. I may see it as green and luscious, whereas to others it may be nothing significant. (*My Isle* critical reflection)

Student feedback for 'Green Worlds' was overwhelmingly positive. In post-course student feedback, 100 per cent felt inspired to learn and the unit had an 83 per cent success or pass rate. In their final journal reflections, one student wrote: 'This subject [unit] has not only opened my eyes to the role nature plays in my life, but also how important it is to reflect on things even if they have the potential to be very confronting … I am so grateful that I took this subject [unit] because it gave me the tools I need to appreciate [nature].' Another reflected: 'I learned so much about nature without ever once feeling like I was learning.' Another student reported that: 'Since starting this subject [unit] I have attempted to become more environmentally friendly and aware.' This student changed her consumer behaviours by recycling soft plastics, purchasing natural products and contributing to non-profit environmental organisations.

The place-based creative activities implemented in this environmental literature unit were built from a learner-centred foundation that focussed on each learner's sense of place. Through this place-based interdisciplinary work, the assessment developed students' personal connection to place and their critical thinking, writing and analytical skills. Critically, it produced the twofold benefit that comes with authentic PBL. Place was both topic and teacher, as Shakespeare was explored through sense of place, and sense of place was enriched through Shakespeare.

Community Engagement and Relational Place

The local is often considered essential to PBL (Demarest, 2015: 42–3; Smith, 2002: 593), but as we have seen, it is also problematic (Section 2). Nonetheless, place is constituted through local interactions, and this relational Mode of place reinforces the importance of community in activating place-based learning (Bartholomaeus, 2013: 20–1). This mode of PBL aligns with anti-racist Shakespeare pedagogy in its community-based approach to education (Dadabhoy & Mehdizadeh, 2023: 14). Educators can connect themes in literary texts to 'cultural and local themes' to enable students to understand 'how texts and contexts work together to make meaning' (Bass et al., 2020: 21–2).

Participation in community theatre is one way for place-based Shakespeare to explore the Practice of community engagement (Figure 13). In my 'Remaking Shakespeare' unit at JCU, students engaged with the region's professional Shakespeare theatre company, TheatreiNQ. Actors and company members visited campus (or, during the COVID-19 pandemic, Zoomed in) for Q & A sessions and special performances. Students were also required, as part of their assessment, to attend a performance of TheatreiNQ's annual 'Shakespeare under the Stars' production and produce an extensive theatre review informed by their learnings in the course. Learners prepared by reading and discussing theatre reviews and scholarly work on the genre (Fisher, 2015). A target publication and audience were provided. This task aligns with Loh's assertion that PBL should 'emphasize literary production' to encourage participation in the production of local culture (2018: n.p.). The theatre review task not only built camaraderie in the class, as students often chose to attend performances together; it also generated interaction between their Shakespeare class and their local community. Further, the design of the assessment task was outward-facing, and one review was published on the Shakespeare Reloaded website.[27] The theatre review heightened the relevance of assessment by grounding it in local events and reinforced links between Shakespeare and the students' location. The impact of this community engagement was made clear in student feedback, which highlighted that the 'best aspects' of the unit were 'the practical elements such as the play we watched and the visits from theatre companies'; 'The addition of workshops by visiting actors and the inclusion of real life elements such as the Othello play into the coursework' (2019 Unit Report). The engagement with the theatre company and the theatre review aligns with Demarest's priorities for

---

[27] Casey Salt, '"Set you down this": A modern *Othello* and the narrative of racism', Shakespeare Reloaded Blog, 10 December 2019, http://shakespearereloaded .edu.au/%E2%80%9Cset-you-down-this%E2%80%9D-modern-othello-and-nar rative-racism.

PBL: it was original, personal and important to others around them (2015: 144). In inviting community artists into the classroom and asking students to venture out into the community, this course explicitly operated in a relational mode, legitimating cultural arts and demonstrating co-constitutive relational interactions between Shakespeare and place.

Virtual Activities and the Multiplicity of Place

This Element was written during a global pandemic, which caused significant difficulties for outdoor and environmental education (Quay et al., 2020).[28] The shift to online-only learning inevitably problematised my work on the potential of place. How might PBL adapt in a virtual environment?

This very question fosters a false dichotomy in a perceived conflict between the proliferation of mobile and digital technologies and 'the widely held belief that environmental learning is best nurtured through direct and "unmediated" sensorial contact with non-human others' (Greenwood & Hougham, 2015: 98). While we might assume that the digital 'comes with an assumption of dematerialization and detachment from a physical location' (Pawlicka-Deger, 2021: 328), our 'embroilment in technology' brings with it 'a genuine, if still not fully understood, phenomenon of place' (Casey, 1997: xii–xiv).

There is extensive scholarship on virtual PBL (Lansiquot & MacDonald, 2019: 5), with literature on the use of technology in environmental education dating to the 1990s (Greenwood & Hougham, 2015: 99). Renata D. Lansiquot and Sean P. MacDonald contend that 'learning in

---

[28] There is extensive work on digital Shakespeare pedagogy which falls outside the scope of this Element. This includes online activities and resources as well as scholarship on digital pedagogy. For an indicative sample of online activities, see the Shakespeare Reloaded open-access online games and activities (www.shakespearereloaded.edu.au) such as Shakespeed (Semler, 2019). Other online tools include myshakespeare.com, wordplayshakespeare.com and Gina Bloom's *Play the Knave* (www.playtheknave.org/). For recent scholarship on digital Shakespeare pedagogy, see Semler, Hansen and Manuel (2023); Henderson and Vitale (2021); Wittek and McInnis (2021); Carson and Kirwan (2014).

virtual worlds by definition is place-based' (2019: 2). The tools of virtual PBL – digital storytelling, mapping (Chin & Swift, 2019), data visualisation, Google Maps (Demarest, 2015: 22), virtual reality (VR), online archives and museums (Lansiquot & MacDonald, 2019: 6) and game design – can 'enhance the exploration of physical place and reimagine the physical in an interdisciplinary environment' (Lansiquot & MacDonald, 2019: 2).

In 2021, I converted an on-campus Shakespeare unit (that had previously involved interactive workshops, outdoor learning and theatre trips) to online learning. We interacted online through Blackboard Ultra's Collaborate and communications platform Slack. To ameliorate the loss of face-to-face learning in a unit devoted to play-texts, I introduced the virtual online platform, Gather.[29] Gather (www.gather.town) is a platform that provides customisable spaces that aim to replicate 'real-life' in-person conversations through providing a sense of bodies in space. Featuring video chat capabilities and video game–esque avatars, Gather enables educators to incorporate movement and space into a class. Users can take advantage of pre-existing customisable templates or can upload unique background images and designs.[30]

Throughout the semester, students came together in our Gather space. I created a rudimentary online space by uploading a photograph of Shakespeare's Globe in London (Figure 16). I added basic props, including a table complete with ink, quill and papers. Students had to navigate to the table using their avatars to access the day's script, which could be opened in a new window, enabling students to simultaneously view the script (for close reading) and traverse the stage space.

Compared to Collaborate and Zoom, Gather offered a wildly different virtual experience for students and for educators: suddenly, movement was a part of the conversation (Figure 16). Information was 'visualized'

[29] My use of this was inspired by its successful implementation by Dr Michael Stevens (University of New South Wales).

[30] Although Gather is designed with educational purposes in mind ('Gather for Education' is a feature of the website), its terms and conditions now regulate the space for users under the age of eighteen. Educators are encouraged to review the conditions in relation to their learners' requirements.

Figure 16 Screenshot of *Othello* tutorial on Gather (2021). Background image of Shakespeare's Globe. Photographer: Pete Le May. Reproduced with permission kindly granted by Gather, Shakespeare's Globe and Pete Le May.

(Lansiquot & MacDonald, 2019: 5). Learners were aware that they occupied a space onstage and that they needed to take other actors into consideration in their decisions and discussions. Explicit and embedded stage directions, proximity, audiences, projection and levels were more readily incorporated into traditional close reading and language analysis.[31] In staging Desdemona's death in *Othello*, one student imported a bed image onto the stage, to facilitate discussion around movement and meaning. This proactive use of space showed that the student felt ownership of the learning environment (Lansiquot & MacDonald, 2019: 5). In a tutorial on Act Three,

---

[31] Students did note a limitation to Gather, as avatars cannot move their hands or perform detailed actions, which prevented the exploration of some stage directions or movements. Movement on Gather is not embodied but transferred to the avatar.

Figure 17 Screenshot of student presentation on Gather (2021). Background image courtesy of Pete Le May and Shakespeare's Globe.

Scene Seven of *King Richard III*, students used the gallery space, and an enthusiastic, detailed discussion of height, power and dynamics ensued. Stage directions such as '*Enter Richard aloft, between two Bishops*' (3.7.93.1SD) were able to be tested and investigated. Buckingham's description of the scene could be visualised:

> Two props of virtue for a Christian prince,
> To stay him from the fall of vanity;
> And see a book of prayer in his hand,
> True ornaments to know a holy man. (*King Richard III*, 3.7.95–98)

As part of their group presentation assessment for the semester, one group decided to use Gather, customising the stage set and performing scenes virtually. Their 'props' included portraits, the white rose and the red, gravestones, mist and a staircase (Figure 17).

Gather also provides opportunities for a less literal engagement with place. To demonstrate its potential for virtual PBL, Lauren Weber and I created Gather spaces for teaching Shakespeare's *A Midsummer Night's*

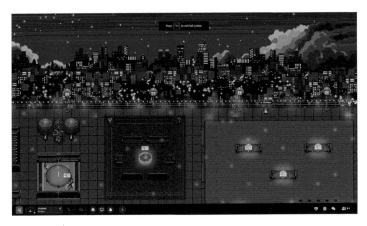

Figure 18 Screenshot of 'Athens' on Gather.

Dream, adapting pre-existing Gather background templates.[32] These Gather spaces enable students to move through some of the play's settings: from Athens to the woods, and into Titania's bower. Throughout, small groups can interact in dedicated areas that enable multiple conversations to take place in one digital space. Students can explore the space independently, finding discussion questions, prompts, activities and scripts.

Our Gather version of the settings of *A Midsummer Night's Dream* begins in a modern urban metropolis (Figure 18). Students enter the space and see a cityscape at night-time, with high-rise buildings visible from a rooftop. This engages learners in a spatial contrast fundamental to the play: 'the sharp Athenian law' (1.1.162) in contrast to the chaotic freedom of the 'wood' with its 'primrose beds' (1.1.214–215). In Athens, students will find private learning spaces with open books – approaching each of these, they can access discussion questions or scripts (these can be

---

[32] If you would like to use these *A Midsummer Night's Dream* Gather spaces, you can download the backgrounds: https://shakespearereloaded.edu.au/shakespeare-and-place-based-learning-gather-background-templates-midsummer-nights-dream

Figure 19 Screenshot of 'The Woods' on Gather.

added or changed by the educator). In groups or individually, students could move through the different learning spaces on the rooftop and engage in different activities. This space alone would provide ample material for at least one class on the play.

When they are ready to move on, students approach a strange, gnarled tree, which looks out of place in the metropolitan setting. This is a portal, allowing a user to enter another space. The portal tree takes students to their next destination: the woods (Figure 19). This mimics the movement of the play from Athens in Act One to the wood in Act Two, which opens with an explicit question about place (not unlike *Macbeth*): 'whither wander you?' (2.1.1). The language of the second act is rich with place beyond the 'grove' itself (2.1.146), from Titania's catalogue of environmental disorder (2.1.81–117) to memories of the 'spiced Indian air' (2.1.124) and Oberon's 'promontory' (2.1.149).

The woods Gather space (Figure 19) features a pleasant generic pastoral setting. A 'green plot' (3.1.3) is visible for the mechanicals' rehearsal. In this open space, there is room for movement and staging. Another portal follows Bottom's journey to Titania's

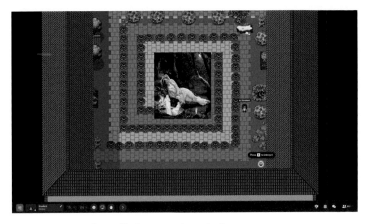

Figure 20 Screenshot of 'The Bower' on Gather.

'flowery bed' (4.1.1) and bower (3.1.188; 3.2.7) (Figure 20). The bower is a smaller, contained space. Here, too, learners can access dialogue from the play.

Gather allows virtual Shakespeare classes to consider movement in space and to contemplate Shakespeare's 'palimpsestic' construction of setting (Markidou, 2016). Not only could educators set up a space for an online class – using templates or starting from scratch – but students too could generate their own virtual places. The potential for learner-centred PBL through platforms like Gather is significant; students could upload images of places significant to them or construct entirely imagined or fictive virtual places that engage their sense of place. This demonstrates the entanglement of dimensions of place; a place-based Shakespeare class will most likely invoke multiple Dimensions and Modes of place – not only setting and imagined and material place but virtual, local and theatrical places as well. While a lesson may emphasise one Dimension or Mode of place, these facets are inseparable parts of a complex whole and always operate in relation to each other.

REFLECTION IN PLACE

Throughout *Shakespeare and Place-Based Learning*, 'Reflection in Place' prompts were offered at the end of each section to generate reflection on the role of place in your Shakespeare pedagogical practice. For this final reflection, I invite you to consider:

- What Dimensions or Modes of place might you incorporate into your Shakespeare classroom?
- What Practices are already a part of your Shakespeare pedagogy?
- This section provides examples of Shakespearean PBL that address the model's twin learning goals. Deepening environmental awareness is a broad learning goal; how might you refine this goal for specific social and environmental concerns in your place?
- Reflect on your understanding of 'sense of place', having explored *Shakespeare and Place-Based Learning*.

The five Practices of PBL explored here – site reading, outdoor education, community engagement, creative and virtual activities – enable educators and learners to interact with different Dimensions and Modes of place, including setting, material and imagined place, relational and eventmental place and place as a form of knowing. In doing so, many other forms of place will be activated: virtual, theatrical, local, more-than-human and Indigenous place. In practice, PBL will never be perfect, and limitations and the unexpected will always emerge. Despite this (or perhaps through this), any place-based work in Shakespeare pedagogy should aim to achieve the four goals identified at the beginning of this section: deepening knowledge of and engagement with Shakespeare's texts; building fundamental skills; expanding a learner's sense of environmental responsibility; and developing a rich, complex sense of place.

Place of Departure: Shakespeare and Identity

Place-based learning is a means to reflect on and learn not only about Shakespeare and our environments but about ourselves as learners and teachers. Places 'are the source of our identities' (Wattchow & Brown, 2011: 12), the 'raw material for the creative production of identity' (Cresswell, 2015: 71) and a lens by which young people begin to make sense of themselves (McInerney et al., 2011: 5). The places we occupy have 'everything to do with what and who we are (and finally, *that* we are)' (Casey, 2009: xiii). Attention to place enables a shift in how we understand identity construction, moving away from an 'individualised' sense of identity to thinking of 'oneself in relation to those others, including human, non-human and earth others, who make up the places we live in' (Somerville et al., 2011: 1). Dramatic literature like Shakespeare can effectively engage students in processes of 'place identity', which refers to 'the way places are involved in the construction of personal and social identities . . . defined as an interpretation of self that uses environmental meaning to symbolise or situate identity' (Anae, 2013: 135–6; see also van de Graaf, 2009: 38). As we have seen, the relationship between Shakespeare and a learner's sense of place is pertinent to their perception of both identity and place.

But the relationship between place and identity is not simple (Wattchow & Brown, 2011: 101). Just as places are complex, dynamic and multiple, so are identities. 'While place and identity are mutually constitutive, notions that suggest that identity is intrinsically tied to place need critical attention' (Charlton et al., 2011: 65). The identities of 'people and places' continually emerge 'as an unfolding, interdependent phenomenon – always evolving, always becoming' (Wattchow & Brown, 2011: 107). Triangulating PBL, identity and Shakespeare reinforces the complexity of our interactions and the high stakes of incorporating place into teaching and learning, especially when aligned with anti-racist Shakespeare pedagogy (Section 1).

Place-based learning is about much more than moving the location of our classrooms: it is centrally interested in the relationship between identity, knowing, becoming and place. Its aims are 'transformational' (Smith, 2017: 18; Somerville et al., 2011: 2). It is not only about using our immediate understanding of place/s. It is this, but it is *also* about a 'radical challenge' (Soja, 1996: 2) to how we conceptualise place. In the words of Soja, we must 'think differently, to expand your geographical imagination beyond its current limits' (1996: 2). Learning with place engages deeper understandings of place, ourselves, Shakespeare and our environmental responsibilities. Place-based learning is an invitation to illuminate Shakespeare through engagement with our sense of place and to radically reimagine our sense of self and place through engagement with Shakespeare.

References

Akhimie, P. (2021). Cultivating expertise: Glossing Shakespeare and race. *Literature Compass*, 18(10), 1–8.

Anae, N. (2013). Athenian and Shakespearean tragedies in Oceania: Teaching dramatic literatures in Fiji. *English Teaching: Practice and Critique*, 12(2), 121–39.

Angulo, A. J. & Schneider, J. (2021). Place, space and localism in education history. *History of Education Quarterly*, 61(4), 389–91.

Argyris, C. & Schön, D. A. (1974). *Theory in Practice: Increasing Professional Effectiveness*. San Francisco, CA: Jossey-Bass Publishers.

Azano, A. (2011). The possibility of place: One teacher's use of place-based instruction for English students in a rural high school. *Journal of Research in Rural Education*, 26(10), 1–12.

Ball, E. L. & Lai, A. (2006). Place-based pedagogy for the arts and humanities. *Pedagogy: Critical Approaches to Teaching Literature, Language, Composition, and Culture*, 6(2), 261–87.

Bartholomaeus, P. (2013). Place-based education and the Australian Curriculum. *Literacy Learning: The Middle Years*, 21(3), 17–23.

Bass, E. L., Azano, A. P. & Callahan, C. M. (2020). A place for writing: Examining a place-based curriculum for high-performing rural writers. *Theory and Practice in Rural Education*, 10(2), 11–25.

Beames, S. (2015). Place-based education: A reconnaissance of the literature. *Pathways: The Ontario Journal of Outdoor Education*, 28(1), 27–30.

Becker, C., Lauterbach, G., Spengler, S., Dettweiler, U. & Mess, F. (2017). Effects of regular classes in outdoor education settings: A systematic review on students' learning, social and health dimensions. *International Journal of Environmental Research and Public Health*, 14(5), 1–20.

Berry, R. (2016). *Shakespeare's Settings and a Sense of Place*. Cardiff: University of Wales Press.

Bertling, J. G. (2018). Non-place and the future of place-based education. *Environmental Education Research*, 24(11), 1627–30.

Biesta, G. & Osberg, D. (eds.) (2010). *Complexity Theory and the Politics of Education*. Rotterdam: Sense Publishers.

Bird Rose, D. & Robin, L. (2004). The ecological humanities in action: An invitation. *Australian Humanities Review* (31–32). https://australianhumanitiesreview.org/2004/04/01/the-ecological-humanities-in-action-an-invitation/.

Bishop, S. (2004). The power of place. *The English Journal*, 93(6), 65–9.

Blatman-Thomas, N. (2019). Reciprocal repossession: Property as land in urban Australia. *Antipode*, 51(5), 1395–415.

Bozio, A. (2020). *Thinking through Place on the Early Modern English Stage*. Oxford: Oxford University Press.

Bruckner, L. & Brayton, D. (eds.) (2011). *Ecocritical Shakespeare*. Farnham: Ashgate.

Buell, L., Heise, U. K. & Thornber, K. (2011). Literature and environment. *The Annual Review of Environment and Resources*, 36, 417–40.

Cameron, J. I. (2014). Learning country: A case study of Australian place-responsive education. In D. A. Gruenewald & G. A. Smith (eds.), *Place-Based Education in the Global Age*. New York: Psychology Press, 283–307.

Carson, C. & Kirwan, P. (eds.) (2014). *Shakespeare and the Digital World: Redefining Scholarship and Practice*. Cambridge: Cambridge University Press.

Carter, P. (1992). *Living in a New Country: History, Travelling and Language*. London: Faber & Faber.

Casey, E. S. (1997). *The Fate of Place: A Philosophical History*. Berkeley: University of California Press.

Casey, E. S. (2009). *Getting Back into Place: Toward a Renewed Understanding of the Place-World*, 2nd ed. Bloomington: Indiana University Press.

Charlton, E., Wyse, D., Cliff Hodges, G. et al. (2011). Place-related identities through texts: From interdisciplinary theory to research agenda. *British Journal of Educational Studies*, 59(1), 63–74.

Chin, T. & Swift, C. (2019). Mapping urban performance culture: Common ground for architecture and theater. In R. D. Lansiquot & S. P. MacDonald (eds.), *Interdisciplinary Perspectives on Virtual Place-Based Learning*. Cham: Palgrave Macmillan, 83–9.

Corbett, M. (2013). Improvisation as a curricular metaphor: Imagining education for a rural creative class. *Journal of Research in Rural Education*, 28(10), 1–11.

Corbett, M. & Donehower, K. (2017). Rural literacies: Toward social cartography. *Journal of Research in Rural Education*, 32(5), 1–13.

Cormack, P. & Green, B. (2007). Writing place in English: How a school subject constitutes children's relations to the environment. *Australian Journal of Language and Literacy*, 30(2), 85–101.

Cresswell, T. (2015). *Place: An Introduction*, 2nd ed. Malden, MA: Wiley-Blackwell.

Dadabhoy, A. (2020). The unbearable whiteness of being (in) Shakespeare. *postmedieval: a journal of medieval cultural studies*, 11(2–3), 228–235.

Dadabhoy, A. & Mehdizadeh, N. (2020). Cultivating an anti-racist pedagogy, in *Folger Critical Race Conversations*, podcast, 10 July. www.youtube.com/watch?v=_4oCWst1cPc&list=PLR8P-dSNaJkXDYEqDI_AX-AKs7J2n Piqc&index=2.

Dadabhoy, A. & Mehdizadeh, N. (2023). *Anti-racist Shakespeare*. Cambridge: Cambridge University Press.

Davis, B. & Sumara, D. (2006). *Complexity and Education: Inquiries into Learning, Teaching, and Research*. New York: Routledge.

Day Fassbinder, S., Nocella, A. J., II & Kahn, R. (eds.) (2012). *Greening the Academy: Ecopedagogy through the Liberal Arts*. Rotterdam: Sense Publishers.

De Barros, E. L. (2019). Teacher trouble: Performing race in the majority-white Shakespeare classroom. *Journal of American Studies*, 54(1), 74–81.

Demarest, A. B. (2015). *Place-Based Curriculum Design: Exceeding Standards through Local Investigations*. New York: Routledge.

Donovan, E. (2016). Learning to embrace our stories: Using place-based education practices to inspire authentic writing. *Middle School Journal*, 47(4), 23–31.

Egan, G. (2006). *Green Shakespeare: From Ecopolitics to Ecocriticism*. London: Routledge.

Egan, G. (2015). *Shakespeare and Ecocritical Theory*. London: Bloomsbury.

Eklund, H. & Hyman, W. B. (eds.) (2019). *Teaching Social Justice through Shakespeare: Why Renaissance Literature Matters Now*. Edinburgh: Edinburgh University Press.

Erickson, P. & Hall, K. F. (2016). 'A new scholarly song': Rereading early modern race. *Shakespeare Quarterly*, 61(1), 1–13.

Escolme, B. (2012). Shakespeare, rehearsal and the site-specific. *Shakespeare Bulletin*, 30(4), 505–22.

Estok, S. C. (2011). *Ecocriticism and Shakespeare: Reading Ecophobia*. London: Palgrave Macmillan.

Evans, N., Whitehouse, H. & Gooch, M. (2012). Barriers, successes and enabling practices of education for sustainability in Far North Queensland schools: A case study. *The Journal of Environmental Education*, 43(2), 121–38.

Fischer, S. (2015). Playing in literary landscapes: Considering children's need for fantasy literature in the place-based classroom. *Occasional Paper Series*, 33, 13–25.

Fisher, M. (2015). *How to Write about Theatre: A Manual for Critics, Students and Bloggers*. London: Bloomsbury Methuen Drama.

Gaard, G. (2009). Children's environmental literature: From ecocriticism to ecopedagogy. *Neohelicon*, 36(2), 321–34.

Gaby, R. (2014). *Open-Air Shakespeare: Under Australian Skies*. Basingstoke: Palgrave.

Gannon, S. (2009a). Into the (textual) west. *English in Australia*, 44(3), 29–37.

Gannon, S. (2009b). Rewriting 'the road to nowhere': Place pedagogies in Western Sydney. *Urban Education*, 44(5), 608–23.

Garrard, G. (2010). Problems and prospects in ecocritical pedagogy. *Environmental Education Research*, 16(2), 233–45.

Gough, N. (2009). How do places *become* 'pedagogical'? In M. Somerville, K. Power & P. de Carteret (eds.), *Landscapes and Learning: Place Studies for a Global World*. Rotterdam: Sense Publishers, 155–73.

Gray, D. (2020). 'Command these elements to silence': Ecocriticism and *The Tempest*. *Literature Compass*, 17(3–4), 1–10.

Green, A. (2013). London in space and time: Peter Ackroyd and Will Self. *English Teaching: Practice and Critique*, 12(2), 28–40.

Green, B. & Clark, U. (2013). Editorial: English(es) and the sense of place: Linguistic and literary landscapes. *English Teaching: Practice and Critique*, 12(2), 1–10.

Green, B., Cormack, P. & Nixon, H. (2007). Introduction: Literacy, place, environment. *The Australian Journal of Language and Literacy*, 30(2), 77–81.

Greenberg, M. (2019). Critically regional Shakespeare. *Shakespeare Bulletin*, 37(3), 341–63.

Greenwood, D. A. (2013). A critical theory of place-conscious education. In R. B. Stevenson, M. Brody, J. Dillon & A. E. J. Wals (eds.), *International Handbook of Research on Environmental Education*. Abingdon: Routledge, 93–100.

Greenwood, D. A. (2019). Place, land, and the decolonization of the settler soul. *The Journal of Environmental Education*, 50(4–6), 358–77.

Greenwood, D. A. & Hougham, R. J. (2015). Mitigation and adaptation: Critical perspectives toward digital technologies in place-conscious environmental education. *Policy Futures in Education*, 13(1), 97–116.

Gruenewald, D. A. (2003a). The best of both worlds: A critical pedagogy of place. *Environmental Education Research*, 14(3), 308–24.

Gruenewald, D. A. (2003b). Foundations of place: A multidisciplinary framework for place-conscious education. *American Educational Research Journal*, 40(3), 619–54.

Gruenewald, D. A. (2014). Place-based education: Grounding culturally responsive teaching in geographical diversity. In D. A. Gruenewald & G. A. Smith (eds.), *Place-Based Education in the Global Age*. New York: Psychology Press, 137–53.

Gruenewald, D. A. & Smith, G. A. (2014a). Afterword: Creating a movement to ground learning in place. In D. A. Gruenewald & G. A. Smith (eds.), *Place-Based Education in the Global Age*. New York: Psychology Press, 345–58.

Gruenewald, D. A. & Smith, G. A. (2014b). Introduction: Making room for the local. In D. A. Gruenewald & G. A. Smith (eds.), *Place-Based Education in the Global Age*. New York: Psychology Press, xiii–xxiii.

Gruenewald, D. A. & Smith, G. A. (eds.) (2014c). *Place-Based Education in the Global Age*. New York: Psychology Press.

Hagood, A. & Price, C. E. (2016). Classroom ecotones: Connecting place-based pedagogy and blended learning. *ISLE: Interdisciplinary Studies in Literature and Environment*, 23(3), 603–25.

Hall, K. F. (1996). Beauty and the beast of whiteness: Teaching race and gender. *Shakespeare Quarterly*, 47(4), 461–75.

Hansen, A. (2021). *Shakespeare in the North: Place, Politics and Performance in England and Scotland*. Edinburgh: Edinburgh University Press.

Hansen, C. (2017). *Shakespeare and Complexity Theory*. London and New York: Routledge.

Hansen, C. (2019). 'Tongues in trees': Reimagining the regions through pastoral place-based pedagogy. *TEXT Journal*, 54, 1–18.

Harris, J.G. (2007). The smell of Macbeth. Shakespeare Quarterly. 58 (4), 465–486.

Henderson, D. H. & Vitale, K. S. (eds.) (2021) *Shakespeare and Digital Pedagogy: Case Studies and Strategies*. London: Bloomsbury.

Hendricks, M. (2019). Coloring the past, rewriting our future: RaceB4Race. *Race and Periodization Symposium*. www.folger.edu/institute/scholarly-programs/race-periodization/margo-hendricks.

hooks, b. (1994). *Teaching to Transgress: Education As the Practice of Freedom*. New York: Routledge.

Huang, A. C. Y. (2007). Shakespearean localities and localities of Shakespeare studies. *Shakespeare Studies*, 35, 186–204.

Hung, R. (2014). In search of ecopedagogy: Emplacing nature in the light of Proust and Thoreau. *Educational Philosophy and Theory*, 46(13), 1387–401.

Hung, R. (2021). Ecopedagogy and education. In *Oxford Research Encyclopedia of Education*. Oxford: Oxford University Press.

James, J. K. & Williams, T. (2017). School-based experiential outdoor education: A neglected necessity. *Journal of Experiential Education*, 40(1), 58–71.

Joubin, A. A. & Starks, L. S. (2021). Teaching Shakespeare in a time of hate. *Shakespeare Survey*, 74, 15–29.

Kahn, R. (2010). *Critical Pedagogy, Ecoliteracy, and Planetary Crisis: The Ecopedagogy Movement*. New York: Peter Lang.

Karim-Cooper, F. (2020). Anti-racist Shakespeare. *Shakespeare's Globe*, 26 May. www.shakespearesglobe.com/discover/blogs-and-features/2020/05/26/anti-racist-shakespeare/.

Karim-Cooper, F. (2021). Shakespeare through decolonization. *English: Journal of the English Association*, 70(271), 319–24.

Kenway, J. (2009). Beyond conventional curriculum cartography via a global sense of place. In M. Somerville, K. Power & P. de Carteret (eds.), *Landscapes and Learning: Place Studies for a Global World*. Rotterdam: Sense Publishers, 195–205.

Kern, R. (2000). Ecocriticism: What is it good for? *Interdisciplinary Studies in Literature and Environment*, 7(1), 9–32.

Kim, M. & Lee, S. (2019). Fostering place attachment through selecting and presenting favorite places. *International Research in Geographical and Environmental Education*, 28(4), 296–308.

Klarer, M. (2011). *An Introduction to Literary Studies*. London: Routledge.

Koessler, C. & Perduca, F. (2019). Critical place pedagogy through tween literature: Educating the gaze to transform spaces into places. In D. L. Banegas, M. Porto, M. López-Barrios & F. Perduca (eds.), *Literature in ELT: Selected Papers from the 44th FAAPI Conference*. Asociación Salteña de Profesores de Inglés (ASPI), 115–24. www.faapi.org.ar/wp-content/uploads/2021/02/FAAPI2019.SelectedPapers.pdf.

Lansiquot, R. D. & MacDonald, S. P. (eds.) (2019). *Interdisciplinary Perspectives on Virtual Place-Based Learning*. Cham: Palgrave Macmillan.

Laroche, R. & Munroe, J. (2019). Teaching environmental justice and early modern texts: Collaboration and connected classrooms. In H. Eklund & W. B. Hyman (eds.), *Teaching Social Justice through Shakespeare: Why Renaissance Literature Matters Now*. Edinburgh: Edinburgh University Press, 124–33.

Lindholdt, P. (1999). Writing from a sense of place. *The Journal of Environmental Education*, 30(4), 4–10.

Loh, C. E. (2018). The poetry of place, the place of poetry: The promise and perils of a place-based literary pedagogy in the Singapore literature classroom. In C. E. Loh, S. S. Choo & C. B. Beavis (eds.), *Literature Education in the Asia-Pacific: Policies, Practices and Perspectives in Global Times*. Abingdon: Routledge, 194–210.

Lowan-Trudeau, G. (2018). Narrating a critical Indigenous pedagogy of place: A literary métissage. *Educational Theory*, 67(4), 509–25.

Marchant, E., Todd, C., Cooksey, R. et al. (2019). Curriculum-based outdoor learning for children aged 9–11: A qualitative analysis of pupils' and teachers' views. *PLoS ONE*, 14(5), e0212242. https://doi.org/10.1371/journal.pone.0212242.

Markidou, V. (2016). William Shakespeare's *Macbeth* as a spatial palimpsest. *Critical Survey*, 28(1), 51–66.

Martin, R. (2015). *Shakespeare and Ecology*. Oxford: Oxford University Press.

Martin, R. & O'Malley, E. (2018). Eco-Shakespeare in performance: Introduction. *Shakespeare Bulletin*, 36(3), 377–90.

Mason, M. (ed.) (2008). *Complexity Theory and the Philosophy of Education*. Malden, MA: Wiley-Blackwell.

Massey, D. (1994). *Space, Place, and Gender*. Minneapolis: University of Minnesota Press.

Massey, D. (2005). *For Space*. London: SAGE Publications.

Mayne, A. (2009). Strange entanglements: Landscapes and historical imagination. In M. Somerville, K. Power & P. de Carteret (eds.), *Landscapes and Learning: Place Studies for a Global World*. Rotterdam: Sense Publishers, 175–93.

McInerney, P., Smyth, J. & Down, B. (2011). 'Coming to a place near you?' The politics and possibilities of a critical pedagogy of place-based education. *Asia-Pacific Journal of Teacher Education*, 39(1), 3–16.

Mentz, S. (2009). *At the Bottom of Shakespeare's Ocean*. London: Continuum.

Mentz, S. (2015). *Shipwreck Modernity: Ecologies of Globalisation, 1550–1719*. Minneapolis: University of Minnesota Press.

Mentz, S. (2019). Shakespeare and the blue humanities. *SEL Studies in English Literature 1500–1900*, 59(2), 383–92.

Minton, G. E. (2018). '. . . the season of all natures': Montana Shakespeare in the Parks' Global Warming *Macbeth*. *Shakespeare Bulletin*, 36(3), 429–48.

Minton, G. E. (2020). *Shakespeare in Montana: Big Sky Country's Love Affair with the World's Most Famous Writer*. Albuquerque: University of New Mexico Press.

Minton, G. E. (2021). Ecological adaptation in Montana: *Timon of Athens* to *Timon of Anaconda*. *New Theatre Quarterly*, 37(1), 20–37.

Misiaszek, G. W. (2018). *Educating the Global Citizen: Understanding Ecopedagogy in Local and Global Contexts*. London: Bloomsbury.

Misiaszek, G. W. (2020). *Ecopedagogy: Critical Environmental Teaching for Planetary Justice and Global Sustainable Development*. London: Bloomsbury.

Monk, N., Chillington Rutter, C., Neelands, J. & Heron, J. (2011). *Open-Space Learning: A Study in Transdisciplinary Pedagogy*. London: Bloomsbury.

Morrison, K. (2002). *School Leadership and Complexity Theory*. London: Routledge.

Morton, T. (2010). *The Ecological Thought*. Cambridge, MA: Harvard University Press.

Moyle, M. (2017). Stepping off the page: Teaching literature with a pedagogy of place. In D. Shannon & J. Galle (eds.), *Interdisciplinary Approaches to Pedagogy and Place-Based Education: From Abstract to the Quotidian*. Cham: Palgrave Macmillan, 105–15.

Mundell, M. (2018). Crafting 'literary sense of place': The generative work of literary place-making. *Journal of the Association for the Study of Australian Literature*, 1(18), 1–17.

Munroe, J. (2015). Shakespeare and ecocriticism revisited. *Literature Compass*, 12(9), 461–70.

Nakagawa, Y. & Payne, P. G. (2017). Educational experiences of post-critical non-place. *International Journal of Qualitative Studies in Education*, 30(2), 147–60.

Orr, D. W. (1992). *Ecological Literacy: Education and the Transition to a Postmodern World*. Albany: State University of New York Press.

Pawlicka-Deger, U. (2021). Place matters: Thinking about spaces for humanities practices. *Arts and Humanities in Higher Education*, 20(3), 320–38.

Potter, E. (2009). Footprints in the Mallee: Climate change, sustaining communities, and the nature of place. In M. Somerville, K. Power & P. de Carteret (eds.), *Landscapes and Learning: Place Studies for a Global World*. Rotterdam: Sense Publishers, 65–74.

Potter, E. & Magner, B. (2018). Australian literature and place-making. *Journal of the Association for the Study of Australian Literature*, 18(1), 1–2.

Potter, E. & Seale, K. (2020). The worldly text and the production of more-than-literary place: Helen Garner's *Monkey Grip* and Melbourne's 'inner north'. *Cultural Geographies*, 27(3), 367–78.

Prieto, E. (2011). Geocriticism, geopoetics, geophilosophy and beyond. In R. T. Tally Jr, (ed.), *Geocritical Explorations: Space, Place, and Mapping in Literary and Cultural Studies*. New York: Palgrave Macmillan, 13–27.

Quay, J., Gray, T., Thomas, G. et al. (2020). What future/s for outdoor and environmental education in a world that has contended with Covid-19? *Journal of Outdoor and Environmental Education*, 23(2), 93–117.

Relph, E. (1976). *Place and Placelessness*. London: Pion.

Renshaw, P. & Tooth, R. (2017). Diverse place-responsive pedagogies: Historical, professional and theoretical threads. In P. Renshaw & R. Tooth (eds.), *Diverse Pedagogies of Place: Educating Students in and for Local and Global Environments*. London: Routledge, 1–21.

Rogers, A., Castree, N. & Kitchin, R. (2013). More-than-human. In *A Dictionary of Human Geography*. Oxford: Oxford University Press. www

.oxfordreference.com/display/10.1093/acref/9780199599868.001.0001/acref-9780199599868-e-1216?rskey=EUGKWq&result=1215.

Scully, A. (2012). Decolonization, reinhabitation and reconciliation: Aboriginal and place-based education. *Canadian Journal of Environmental Education*, 17, 148–58.

Semler, L. E. (2013). *Teaching Shakespeare and Marlowe: Learning versus the System*. London: Bloomsbury.

Semler, L. E. (2016). Prosperous teaching and the thing of darkness: Raising a *Tempest* in the classroom. *Cogent Arts and Humanities*, 3(1), 1–10.

Semler, L. E. (2017a). The Ken Watson Address – seeds of time, section 1: SysEd and the leviathan of learning. *Metaphor*, 1, 8–14.

Semler, L. E. (2017b). The seeds of time, section 2: Presentism and selfie culture. *Metaphor*, 2, 5–13.

Semler, L. E. (2017c). The seeds of time, section 3: Macbeth reading against extinction. *Metaphor*, 4, 4–14.

Semler, L. E. (2019). Shakespeeding into *Macbeth* and *The Tempest*: Teaching with the Shakespeare Reloaded website. In S. Homan (ed.), *How and Why We Teach Shakespeare: College Teachers and Directors Share How They Explore the Playwright's Work with Their Students*. New York: Routledge, 119–27.

Semler, L. E., Hansen, C. & Manuel, J. (eds.) (2023). *Reimagining Shakespeare Education: Teaching and Learning through Collaboration*. Cambridge: Cambridge University Press.

Shakespeare, W. (1995). *King Henry V*. Edited by T. W. Craik. London: Arden Shakespeare.

Shakespeare, W. (1997). *King Lear*. Edited by R. A. Foakes. London: Arden Shakespeare.

Shakespeare, W. (2006). *As You Like It*. Edited by J. Dusinberre. London: Arden Shakespeare.

Shakespeare, W. (2009). *King Richard III*. Edited by J. R. Siemon. London: Arden Shakespeare.

Shakespeare, W. (2011). *The Tempest*. Edited by V. Mason Vaughan & A. T. Vaughan. London: Bloomsbury.

Shakespeare, W. (2015). *Macbeth*. Edited by S. Clark & P. Mason. London: Bloomsbury.

Shakespeare, W. (2016a). *Hamlet*. Edited by A. Thompson & N. Taylor. London: Bloomsbury.

Shakespeare, W. (2016b). *Othello*. Edited by E. A. J. Honigmann & A. Thompson. London: Bloomsbury.

Shakespeare, W. (2017). *A Midsummer Night's Dream*. Edited by S. Chaudhuri. London: Bloomsbury.

Shakespeare, W. (2021). *The Arden Shakespeare Third Series Complete Works*. Edited by R. Proudfoot, A. Thompson, D. S. Kastan & H. R. Woudhuysen. London: Bloomsbury.

Shannon, D. & Galle, J. (2017). Where we are: Place, pedagogy and the outer limits. In D. Shannon & J. Galle (eds.), *Interdisciplinary Approaches to Pedagogy and Place-Based Education: From Abstract to the Quotidian*. Cham: Palgrave Macmillan, 1-8.

Smith, G. A. (2002). Place-based education: Learning to be where we are. *Phi Delta Kappan*, 83(8), 584–94.

Smith, G. A. (2017). Place-based education. In *Oxford Research Encyclopedia of Education*. Oxford: Oxford University Press.

Smith, G. A. & Stevenson, R. B. (2017). Sustaining education for sustainability in turbulent times. *The Journal of Environmental Education*, 48(2), 79–95.

Soja, E. W. (1996). *Thirdspace: Journeys to Los Angeles and Other Real-and-Imagined Places*. Malden, MA: Blackwell Publishers.

Somerville, M. (2010). A place pedagogy for 'global contemporaneity'. *Educational Philosophy and Theory*, 42(3), 326–44.

Somerville, M., Davies, B., Power, K., Gannon, S. & de Carteret, P. (eds.) (2011). *Place Pedagogy Change*. Rotterdam: Sense Publishers.

Somerville, M., Power, K. & de Carteret, P. (eds.) (2009). *Landscapes and Learning: Place Studies for a Global World*. Rotterdam: Sense Publishers.

Stead, V. C. & Altman, J. C. (eds.) (2019). *Labour Lines and Colonial Power: Indigenous and Pacific Island Labour Mobility in Australia*. Canberra: Australian National University Press.

Sterling Brown, D. (2020). 'Hood feminism': Whiteness and segregated (premodern) scholarly discourse in the post-racial era. *Literature Compass*, 18(10), 1–15.

Stevenson, R. B. (2008). A critical pedagogy of place and the critical place(s) of pedagogy. *Environmental Education Research*, 14(3), 353–60.

Tally Jr, R. T. (ed.) (2011). *Geocritical Explorations: Space, Place, and Mapping in Literary and Cultural Studies*. New York: Palgrave Macmillan.

Thompson, A. (ed.) (2021). *The Cambridge Companion to Shakespeare and Race*. Cambridge: Cambridge University Press.

Thompson, A. & Turchi, L. (2016). *Teaching Shakespeare with Purpose: A Student-Centred Approach*. London: Bloomsbury.

Thompson, A. & Turchi, L. (2021). Active Shakespeare: A social justice framework. In D. Ruiter (ed.), *The Arden Handbook of Shakespeare and Social Justice*. London: Bloomsbury, 47–59.

Thompson, R. L. (2013). 'Somewhere and not anywhere': A place-conscious study of literature set in the city of New Orleans. MA thesis, Wake Forest University.

Thurman, C. (2014). *South African Essays on 'Universal' Shakespeare*. London: Routledge.

Tranter, J. (2013). Indigenous Country explained. *Education*, 94(7), 11.

Trinidad, A. M. O. (2011). Sociopolitical development through critical indigenous pedagogy of place: Preparing native Hawaiian young adults to become change agents. *Hulili: Multidisciplinary Research on Hawaiian Well-Being*, 7, 185–221.

Trinidad, A. M. O. (2012). Critical Indigenous pedagogy of place: A framework to indigenize a youth food justice movement. *Journal of Indigenous Social Development*, 1(1), 1–17.

Trinidad, A. M. O. (2014). Critical Indigenous pedagogy of place: How centering Hawaiian epistemology and values in practice affects people on ecosystemic levels. *Journal of Ethnic and Cultural Diversity in Social Work*, 23(2), 110–28.

van de Graaf, P. (2009). *Out of Place? Emotional Ties to the Neighbourhood in Urban Renewal in the Netherlands and the United Kingdom*. Amsterdam: University of Amsterdam Press.

van Gelderen, B. (2017). Growing our own: A 'two way', place-based approach to Indigenous initial teacher education in remote Northern Territory. *Australian and International Journal of Rural Education*, 27(1), 14–28.

Walker-Gibbs, B. (2013). The country's not what it used to be: Research participants' understandings of space, place and identity in rural Victoria. In W. Midgley, P. A. Dahaer & M. Baguley (eds.), *The Role of Participants in Education Research: Ethics, Epistemologies, and Methods*. New York: Routledge, 126–39.

Wallis, L., Hornblow, M., Smit, N. et al. (2021). From little things, big things grow: Building connections through place-based education in the Tasmanian Midlands biodiversity hotspot. *Ecological Management & Restoration*, 22(2), 152–63.

Watson, R. N. (2008). *Back to Nature: The Green and the Real in the Late Renaissance*. Philadelphia: University of Pennsylvania Press.

Wattchow, B. & Brown, M. (2011). *A Pedagogy of Place: Outdoor Education for a Changing World*. Clayton: Monash University Publishing.

Westphal, B. (2011). Foreword. In R. T. Tally Jr, (ed.), *Geocritical Explorations: Space, Place, and Mapping in Literary and Cultural Studies*. New York: Palgrave, ix–xv.

Whitehouse, H., Watkin Lui, F., Sellwood, J., Barrett, M. J. & Chigeza, P. (2014). Sea Country: Navigating Indigenous and colonial ontologies in Australian environmental education. *Environmental Education Research*, 20(1), 56–69.

Wittek, S. & McInnis, D. (eds.) (2021). *Shakespeare and Virtual Reality*. Cambridge: Cambridge University Press.

Woodhouse, J. L. & Knapp, C. E. (2000). Place-based curriculum and instruction. Educational Resources Information Center (ERIC) Document Reproduction Service No. EDO-RC00-6. https://files.eric.ed.gov/fulltext/ED448012.pdf.

Wyse, D., Nikolajeva, M., Charlton, E. et al. (2012). Place-related identity, texts, and transcultural meanings. *British Educational Research Journal*, 38(6), 1019–39.

Wyse, L. (2021). *Ecospatiality: A Place-Based Approach to American Literature*. Iowa City: University of Iowa Press.

Yachnin, P. (2019). *The Tempest: Critical Introduction*. https://internetshakespeare.uvic.ca/doc/Tmp_GenIntro/index.html.

Yunkaporta, T. (2009). Aboriginal pedagogies at the cultural interface. PhD thesis, James Cook University. http://eprints.jcu.edu.au/10974/.

Acknowledgements

Education is innately collaborative, and this Element was created thanks to the contributions of many students and colleagues. Thank you to the students at James Cook University (JCU) and in high schools throughout Townsville for inspiring me with your engagement and originality. Thank you to Nola Alloway and my colleagues at JCU for providing support for this project and to Heather Fraser for welcoming me into the local teaching community. Thank you to TheatreiNQ, especially Terri Brabon and Arminelle Fleming, for being a part of this project and for sharing your expertise. Thank you to Chrissy Maguire for your beautiful photography. To Liam Semler and the Shakespeare Reloaded family, thank you for creating a space for ongoing collegial innovation in Shakespeare education. Thanks to Dr Lauren Weber for your friendship and insightful assistance with this project. Thank you also to my wonderful Australian National University (ANU) colleagues and students. I would like to thank Paul Prescott for his insightful, generous review of an earlier version of this Element, which was invaluable in finalising it. To my family, thank you for teaching me my love of place. And to Michael, thank you for making 'place' a home.

This Element was created in the unceded lands of the Bindal, Wulgurukaba, Gadigal, Ngunnawal and Ngambri peoples. In the spirit of reconciliation, I acknowledge these Traditional Custodians of Country throughout Australia and their connections to land, sea and community.

Cambridge Elements ☰

Shakespeare and Pedagogy

Liam E. Semler

University of Sydney

Liam E. Semler is Professor of Early Modern Literature in the
Department of English at the University of Sydney.
He is author of *Teaching Shakespeare and Marlowe: Learning
versus the System* (2013) and co-editor (with Kate Flaherty and
Penny Gay) of *Teaching Shakespeare beyond the Centre:
Australasian Perspectives* (2013). He is editor of *Coriolanus: A
Critical Reader* (2021) and co-editor (with Claire Hansen and
Jackie Manuel) of *Reimagining Shakespeare Education:
Teaching and Learning through Collaboration* (Cambridge,
forthcoming). His most recent book outside Shakespeare
studies is *The Early Modern Grotesque: English Sources and
Documents 1500–1700* (2019). Liam leads the Better Strangers
project which hosts the open-access Shakespeare Reloaded
website (shakespearereloaded.edu.au).

Gillian Woods

Birkbeck College, University of London

Gillian Woods is Reader in Renaissance Literature and Theatre
at Birkbeck College, University of London. She is the author of
Shakespeare's Unreformed Fictions (2013; joint winner of
Shakespeare's Globe Book Award), *Romeo and Juliet: A
Reader's Guide to Essential Criticism* (2012), and numerous
articles about Renaissance drama. She is the co-editor
(with Sarah Dustagheer) of *Stage Directions and Shakespearean
Theatre* (2018). She is currently working on a new edition of

A Midsummer Night's Dream for Cambridge University Press, as well as a Leverhulme-funded monograph about Renaissance Theatricalities. As founding director of the Shakespeare Teachers' Conversations, she runs a seminar series that brings together university academics, school teachers and educationalists from non-traditional sectors, and she regularly runs workshops for schools.

ADVISORY BOARD

Janelle Jenstad, *University of Victoria*

Farah Karim-Cooper, *Shakespeare's Globe*

Bi-qi Beatrice Lei, *National Taiwan University*

Florence March, *Université Paul-Valéry Montpellier*

Peggy O'Brien, *Folger Shakespeare Library*

Paul Prescott, *University of California Merced*

Abigail Rokison-Woodall, *University of Birmingham*

Emma Smith, *University of Oxford*

Patrick Spottiswoode, *Shakespeare's Globe*

Jenny Stevens, *English Association*

Ayanna Thompson, *Arizona State University*

Joe Winston, *University of Warwick*

ABOUT THE SERIES

The teaching and learning of Shakespeare around the world is complex and changing. Elements in Shakespeare and Pedagogy synthesises theory and practice, including provocative, original pieces of research, as well as dynamic, practical engagements with learning contexts.

Cambridge Elements ☰

Shakespeare and Pedagogy

Printed in the United States
by Baker & Taylor Publisher Services